NAFTA
MANAGING THE
CULTURAL DIFFERENCES

NAFTA

MANAGING THE
CULTURAL DIFFERENCES

ROBERT T. MORAN
JEFFREY ABBOTT

Gulf Publishing Company
Houston, London, Paris, Zurich, Tokyo

NAFTA
MANAGING THE
CULTURAL DIFFERENCES

Gulf Publishing Company
Book Division
P.O. Box 2608, Houston, Texas 77252-2608

10 9 8 7 6 5 4 3 2 1

Library of Congress Cataloging-in-Publication Data
Moran, Robert T., 1938–
    NAFTA : managing the cultural differences / Robert T.
Moran, Jeffrey D. Abbott.
        p.   cm.
    Includes bibliographical references and index.
    ISBN 0-88415-500-5
    1. Free trade—North America.   2. North America—
Foreign economic relations.   3. Intercultural
communication—North America.   4. Canada. Treaties, etc.
1992 Oct. 7.   I. Abbott, Jeffrey D.   II. Title.
HF1746.M67 1994
382'.917—dc20   94-12482
                                                              CIP

DEDICATION

To my father Robert C. Moran who at eighty-six is intellectually sharp, challenging assumptions and letting little go by without his critique.

Robert T. Moran

To my parents Elmer and Nancy Abbott for their love, support, and encouragement, and to the students of International Business at the ITESM, Campus Monterrey, for their friendship and hospitality. You will always be welcome in my home.

Jeffrey D. Abbott

Contents

Acknowledgments

We wish to acknowledge and thank the following persons for their important contributions to this book.

Shoshana B. Tancer for her offers of assistance and for providing good material in Chapter One and the United States Resource section.

Our subject experts and colleagues who wrote several important sections of the book.

Jennifer Hamilton for her help as research assistant.

John K. Barrett, Executive Director of the American Chamber of Commerce of Mexico, Monterrey.

J. Ian Burchett, Canadian Consul and Trade Commissioner in Canada.

John A. Harris, U.S. Commercial Consul in Monterrey, and Jan Fedorowicz of Prospectus Publications, Ltd.

Juan Garcia Sordo, Director of the Department of International Business, ITESM.

William J. Lowe, Editor-in-Chief of Gulf Publishing Company, who is always a pleasure to work with, and Joyce Alff, whose skills we appreciate.

Eva Kras, an expert on Mexico, who suggested an important perspective that was missing.

Judith E. Soccorsy for her significant contributions to this book.

Foreword

Rafael Rangel-Sostmann, Ph.D.
President
Instituto Tecnologico y de Estudios
Superiores de Monterrey, Mexico

Geography has placed Mexico, the USA, and Canada side by side, but stronger ties will come about through mutual understanding and acceptance of our cultural diversity. NAFTA's success cannot be based on economics alone. With the increasing contact and interaction that this step towards economic integration is bringing, understanding between the people of our three countries has become equally essential. This is where the importance of this book lies. It makes clear the need to comprehend and appreciate our divergent cultures if we are to work together effectively for mutual benefit.

Foreword

Richard D. Mahoney
Secretary of State
State of Arizona

The New World came about from the fracture of three empires. The North American Free Trade Agreement now anticipates a new trade and capital communion between Mexico, Canada, and the United States—one that hopes to transcend two centuries of division and, in the Mexican-American case, deep suspicion. Left out of the conventional cost-benefit calculation of NAFTA, however, is the human dimension involved in making it work.

NAFTA: Managing the Cultural Differences conveys an essential message about the human dimension: without a new level of cultural comprehension and engagement between the American peoples, trade and capital opportunities will be lost. My Thunderbird colleagues and friend, Dr. Robert Moran, and his co-author, Jeffrey Abbott, have floated a new currency of sorts—beyond the dollar and the peso—by identifying the key components of managing cultural differences inherent in NAFTA. They have provided a brief on the legal framework, the historical evolution of the agreement, as well as the modalities of human resource transfer among the countries and tactics of intercultural negotiation. Their use of case studies and hypothetical examples is unusually illuminating.

As an elected official from a state that borders Mexico, I am especially concerned about the possibilities and vulnerabilities of an open border. William Grieder's characterization of the environmental impact of border trade as "a 2,000-mile-long Love Canal" may be rank caricature, but it captures the depth of popular anxiety. The flood of drugs and aliens are far more real and far more immediate threats.

This is why NAFTA is so important and why it must be managed so aggressively: it *can* become a counter-magnet to illegal immigration; it *can* spur huge growth in American exports in everything from pharmaceuticals to Alphagraphics; it *can* tap bicultural richness across a border that for 150 years has demarcated, not just divided ground and divided language, but divided humanity.

The Mexican poet and essayist Octavio Paz once wrote that America and Mexico lived within "a labyrinth of solitude," lost not only to each other but to the chance of casting off their traditional roles of the dominant and the dependent. The reawakening at hand is not just with Canada and Mexico; it is with ourselves.

Introduction

In October 1993, I had just returned from Monterrey, Mexico where I had the honor of being invited, along with Dr. Carla Hills, NAFTA Trade Negotiator; Dr. Dominick Salavatore; Ing. Rodrigo Guerra; Donald Campbell; Dr. Jaime Mario Willars; E. Lic. Sandra Fuentes, and others to participate in the Second Symposium at the Monterrey Institute of Technology. Each presenter made a presentation to about 1,100 students, faculty, and business people.

While in Monterrey, I became acquainted with Jeff Abbott, a graduate of Thunderbird, who is now a faculty member of the Monterrey Institute of Technology and one of the conference organizers. We discussed the possibility of writing a book on NAFTA. At that time, we had a strong belief that NAFTA would pass. The focus of our proposed book was clear—for NAFTA to succeed the people involved (Canadians, Americans and Mexicans) must understand each other. Because of the cross-cultural environment of NAFTA, a knowledge of each country's customs, business culture, and negotiating variables would be necessary. I was the only speaker to present this perspective at the symposium in October. Most of the other presenters focused on the economic and political perspectives that obviously are of significance.

After returning to Arizona, I called my eighty-six-year-old Canadian father who is slower physically than he was thirty years ago, but mentally just as sharp. The conversation with my father went something like this: "What were you doing in Mexico?" he asked. "I gave a little speech on NAFTA," I answered.

My father's response surprised me. "Did you try to kill it?" he asked, and then continued. "Our Prime Minister said he would kill it." My dad and I moved to other topics, but the conversation determined my decision to write something constructive on NAFTA for persons in Canada, the United States, and Mexico. (This book will be available in Spanish and French.)

The authors of this book are fully aware of the limitations of our approach. Our first consideration is that, at the time this book goes to press, Mexico is in transition. The March 23, 1994 assassination of Luis Donaldo Colosio, the political heir of President Carlos Salinas de Gortari in the Institutional Revolutionary Party (PRI) sent Mexican politics into chaos. Ernesto Zedillo was named as the PRI's candidate, but is not considered a certain winner in the August 21, 1994 elections.

We also realize a significant percentage of the Mexican population is poor and over 20 percent live in extreme poverty. Any picture drawn of Mexico is, of course, incomplete without those components and many others as well. Most experts also believe that small and medium-sized Mexican businesses need to benefit from NAFTA. If the upper class only benefits from NAFTA, the consequences of social unrest increase and all of us involved have shirked our responsibilities.

The Mexican cases and much of the Mexican material in this book are drawn from business experiences in Monterrey and Mexico City. This is also a limitation to our approach. We believe, however, that trade between nations is an essential ingredient in the betterment of the lives of all people of any country.

However, *NAFTA: Managing the Cultural Differences* is directed to business persons and students who are interested in ways in which our global economy is becoming more interdependent, as well as those persons who wish to participate in the additional opportunities now available.

It was a pleasure collaborating with Jeff Abbott, a serious scholar and excellent teacher. Without exception, the talented individuals we asked to share their expertise with us, did so willingly and enthusiastically. Each is identified in the Acknowledgments or in specific chapters.

We hope this book will help each reader understand NAFTA and the Canadian, American, and Mexican individuals who will help make it work.

Robert T. Moran

NAFTA
MANAGING THE
CULTURAL DIFFERENCES

The NAFTA Challenge

The Prime Minister of Canada, Jean Chrétien, relayed the following story: "We were making jokes here at the time that Mulroney (a former Prime Minister of Canada) would say 'yes' to Bush even before the telephone would ring. I say that at least he should have waited until the telephone rang to say 'yes'" [1].

In February 1977, after Mexico discovered significant reserves of oil and gas, President Carter visited Mexico. The following are excerpts from the speeches made by President José López Portillo of Mexico and President Jimmy Carter of the United States [2].

President López Portillo:

It has been two years now since we met for the first time. Since then, a great deal of water has flowed beneath the bridges of the Rio Grande. A great deal also has happened within our countries and between our countries, as it has in the world and to the world. . . .

. . . Among permanent, not casual neighbors, surprise moves and sudden deceit or abuse are poisonous fruits that sooner or later have a reverse effect.

Mexico has thus suddenly found itself the center of American attention—attention that is a surprising mixture of interest, disdain, and fear, much like the recurring vague fears you yourselves inspire in certain areas of our national subconscious.

Most of the material in Chapter One was written by Shoshana B. Tancer, Professor of International Studies and Director of the NAFTA Center at the American Graduate School of International Management, Glendale, Arizona. As an attorney and academician, she is a recognized expert on NAFTA.

Let us seek only lasting solutions—good faith and fair play—nothing that would make us lose the respect of our children.

Response by President Carter:

President López Portillo and I have, in the short time together on this visit, found that we have many things in common. We both represent great nations; we both have found an interest in archeology; we both must deal with difficult questions like energy and the control of inflation . . . we both have beautiful and interesting wives; and we both run several kilometers every day. As a matter of fact, I told President López Portillo that I first acquired my habit of running here in Mexico City. My first running course was from the Palace of Fine Arts to the Majestic Hotel, where my family and I were staying.

In the midst of the Folklorico performance, I discovered that I was afflicted with Montezuma's revenge.

President Portillo's eloquent and candid perspective appear to be trivialized and not understood by President Carter.

The three countries of NAFTA share much in common. Canada and the United States share a 5,527 mile open land border. The United States exports more to Canada than it does to Japan, Mexico, and Europe combined. Mexico and the United States share a shorter land border that is fenced and patrolled. The trade between the United States and Mexico is significantly increasing each year.

Between Canada and Mexico is the United States. Trade between Canada and Mexico is at an all time high. A Mexican colleague recently said, "We in Mexico have more in common with Canada than with the United States."

On June 30, 1993, the Canadian Parliament approved the North American Free Trade Agreement. It was approved by the Congress of the United States on November 18, 1993, and by the Mexican Congress on November 22, 1993. NAFTA is real.

This book is about helping individuals in the three countries make NAFTA work for them. Our premise, and an underlying assumption of the book, is that cross-cultural and global competencies are crucial for the success of the individuals involved in NAFTA.

We begin with some preliminaries, including demographics and import and export information of the three countries (Tables 1-1 and 1-2).

To contextualize NAFTA, one must go back eight years to the beginning of free trade talks and negotiations between the United States and Canada. This chronology is sparse on detail; obviously much work and struggle took place between the highlighted dates.

Chronology of Free Trade Agreement (FTA) and North American Free Trade Agreement (NAFTA)

The Beginning: Canada and the United States

March 1985

President Ronald Reagan and Canadian Prime Minister Brian Mulroney meet and agree to explore the possibilities for reducing and eliminating trade barriers.

September 1985

President Reagan and Prime Minister Mulroney exchange letters of resolution to negotiate a Free Trade Agreement (FTA).

(text continued on page 6)

Table 1-1
Trade Figures, 1991 (In Billions of U.S. Dollars)

	CANADA	MEXICO	UNITED STATES
MEXICO			
Exports	2.3		31.9
Imports	0.4		33.3
UNITED STATES			
Exports	82.5	33.3	
Imports	95.6	31.9	
CANADA			
Exports		0.4	95.6
Imports		2.3	82.5

Table 1-2
Demographics of Canada, Mexico, and the United States

	CANADA	MEXICO	UNITED STATES
Population (1992)	27,351,000	89,000,000	256,560,000
Population growth rate (natural)	0.7%	2%	0.5%
Ethnic divisions	British: 25% French: 24% other European: 16% Indigenous: 1.5% Mixed: 28%	Mestizo: 60% Indigenous: 29% White: 9%	White: 85% Black: 12% Other: 3%
Religion	Roman Catholic: 46% Protestant: 41%	Roman Catholic: 97% Protestant: 3%	Roman Catholic 25% Protestant 61%

	English French	Spanish	English
Languages	English French	Spanish	English
Literacy	99%	90%	97%
Labor force	Services: 28% Manufacturing: 52% Agricultural: 4%	Services: 45% Manufacturing: 19% Primary: 16%	Services: 34% Manufacturing: 17% Agricultural: 3%
Age Distribution			
0–14	21%	37%	22%
15–59	63%	58%	61%
60 +	16%	6%	17%
Urban population	77%	72%	76%

Source: *1994 World Almanac and Book of Facts,* 1994 Funk & Wagnalls Corp.

5

(text continued from page 3)

October 1987

U.S. and Canadian negotiators sign a draft of the Agreement.

December 1987

The heads of both delegations ratify the text of the Agreement. The final version is sent to the United States Congress and the Canadian Parliament.

January 1989

The FTA between the United States and Canada goes into effect.

Mexico Joins Discussions
April 1990

The Mexican Senate establishes a forum for consultations on the FTA.

June 1990

The United States Senate opens hearings on a "fast track" bill that would allow President George Bush to negotiate directly with President Carlos Salinas, and the two Presidents issue a joint communiqué announcing their intention to negotiate an FTA.

September 1990

Canada, the United States, and Mexico agree to negotiate a free trade agreement.

February 1991

President Salinas, President Bush, and Prime Minister Mulroney agree to start trilateral negotiations for a North American FTA.

June 1991

Trilateral negotiations between Canada, Mexico, and the United States open in Toronto, Canada.

August 12, 1992

NAFTA negotiations completed.

September 18, 1992

President Bush formally notified Congress of his intention to enter into the Agreement.

November 1992

Bill Clinton wins the U.S. Presidential election.

December 17, 1992

President Bush, President Salinas, and Prime Minister Mulroney sign the NAFTA.

Spring 1993

Negotiation begins for the side agreements promised by Clinton in his campaign.

June 1993

Canadian Parliament approves the Agreement, Prime Minister Mulroney proclaims it and steps down from office.

June 30, 1993

U.S. District Court declares that NAFTA will be illegal as the Executive Branch did not conduct a full environmental impact study on the results of the Agreement.

August 13, 1993

Side Agreements are completed in principle.

October 12, 1993

Side Agreements texts are made public.

November 18, 1993

U. S. Congress approves NAFTA.

November 22, 1993

Mexican Congress approves NAFTA.

January 1, 1994

NAFTA implemented.

Pros and Cons

Like most issues that have an emotional edge, the passage of NAFTA was debated to a greater or lesser degree by perhaps every American, Mexican, and Canadian. Many doomsayers vehemently argued their impassioned positions, citing the fear of job loss and low wages, more damage to struggling U.S. and Canadian economies, and the continued deterioration of the environment among reasons not to support the agreement. To further solidify positions, billionaire H. Ross Perot and Vice President Al Gore took to the airwaves to crystalize public opinion and add fuel for the fire.

Conversely, big business in Mexico, Canada, and the United States, hopeful of expanded opportunities for increased trade and the growth and development of possible manufacturing sites, supported the forthcoming ratification of NAFTA. Business coughed up large amounts of dollars to lobby for the passage of NAFTA. *The New York Times* [3] estimated pro-NAFTA forces spending between $5 million and $30 million—understandable when 86 percent of *Fortune* magazine's top 500 manufacturers have operations in Mexico [4].

NAFTA in Summary

The North American Free Trade Agreement is unique. It is the first trade agreement entered into between industrial countries and a developing nation, and the first trade agreement that includes intellectual property, labor rights, and the environment. It should be noted from the outset that a trade agreement is an agreement that permits the nations who are signatories to decrease tariffs or custom duties on trade between or among themselves within a reasonable period of time. Such agreements are possible with the present rules regarding international trade, provided that the member nations do not raise existing tariffs for non-member nations. Free trade agreements do not create common markets for they do not permit the free movement of people. Historically, free trade agreements have allowed for the free trade of goods.

The Canada–U.S. Free Trade Agreement (FTA), the precursor for NAFTA, became operational January 1, 1989. That agreement

Table 1-3
Supporters and Detractors

	SUPPORTERS	DETRACTORS
CANADA	• Conservative Party • Big Business	• New Democratic Party • Citizens' Concerned About Free Trade • Labor Unions • Environmentalists
MEXICO	• Institutional Revolutionary Party (PRI) • Big Business • Party of National Action (PAN)	• Catholic Bishops • Small and medium-sized companies
UNITED STATES	• Republican Party • Big business • Latino business people	• Labor Unions • Ralph Nader • Environmentalists • H. Ross Perot • Jesse Jackson • Black Caucuses • Blue collar workers

broke new ground by including services and providing new mechanisms for dispute resolution. The years of experience Canada and the United States had in implementing their agreement made it possible to fine-tune some terms in NAFTA, such as how to determine whether specific goods were indeed of Canadian, Mexican, or U.S. origin or to determine the procedures to be followed in the event of trade dispute. Having a framework in place enabled the negotiators to proceed quickly to discuss substantive matters and achieve consensus.

However, NAFTA is still a very complex document. When Perot challenged his critics by asking whether they had read the Agreement, he was asking the wrong question. The better question should have been whether having read it, they understood what was written.

The North American Free Trade Agreement is a long document. Its text alone comprises over a thousand pages, and there are a number of annexes that are as long. The Agreement is divided into eight parts: Part 1: General; Part 2: Trade in Goods; Part 3: Technical Barriers to Trade; Part 4: Government Procurement; Part 5: Investment, Services, and Related Matters; Part 6: Intellectual Property; Part 7: Administrative and Institutional Provisions; and Part 8: Other Provisions. There is a separate volume that deals with the "rules of origin," i.e., how to determine whether a product is eligible for preferential treatment accorded goods from the NAFTA nations. Three additional volumes are detailed tariff schedules, one for each member country.

Before focusing on the various sectors that are impacted by NAFTA, it should be stated that many claim that NAFTA is a misnomer, that it is not really a free trade agreement but rather an investment agreement. It establishes the principle of "national treatment" not only for trade, but guarantees that service providers also will have the right to invest and provide services in the other nations, as if they were nationals, although there is a phase-in period. Investors also are protected by the principles of non-discriminatory treatment. These principles include free transfer of capital for investment purposes, freedom from performance requirements (e.g., Mexico previously demanded a percentage of export before sales were permitted in the domestic market in the automotive sector), limited exercise of the sovereign right of expropriation, (i.e., the process of taking property must conform with established international legal principles), and finally, the use of international arbitration rather than a nation's courts to settle trade disputes if violation of the Agreement is alleged.

In overview, the following are the principal features of the trading relationship among the three nations under NAFTA.

Trade in Goods

Tariffs

All internal tariffs will be reduced to zero at the end of 15 years for trade between the United States, Canada, and Mexico. Based on the Canada–U.S. Free Trade Agreement (FTA), all tariffs on goods moving between those two countries will end in

1998. As relates to trade with Mexico, tariffs for those items that require a longer adjustment period, primarily agricultural goods, will remain in place for approximately 15 years.

Goods are classified into general categories. The "A" category includes goods for which tariffs were removed entirely as of January 1, 1994, such as computers, telecommunications, aerospace equipment, and medical products. In the "B" category, tariffs diminish at the rate of 20 percent a year for five years, and in the "C" category they diminish by 10 percent a year for ten years. The "C+" category is composed of goods for which tariffs diminish for the next 15 years in equal annual reductions. These goods include glassware, orange juice, peanuts, sugar, and watches. It is believed that 65 percent of U.S. goods entering Mexico will be at zero tariff within five years. It should be noted that prior to the passage of NAFTA, the average U.S. tariff was 4 percent for goods being imported from Mexico, whereas the average Mexican tariff was 10 percent. There are provisions in the Agreement that provide for the accelerated reduction of tariffs on a number of goods, including flat glass.

Reservations or exceptions were made by each of the three nations to protect sensitive sectors. Mexico would not negotiate regarding investment in petroleum and basic petrochemicals based on the constitutional provisions that declare petroleum as belonging to the state. Canada, concerned about protecting cultural identity, retained the right to ban materials/services that would infringe on Canadian identity, such as objectionable radio and television programs, movies, and print media. The United States protected farmers by demanding the right to maintain price supports.

Rules of Origin

There was considerable fear that NAFTA would enable one or more of the member nations to be used as export platforms for goods that were from outside of the region. For example, the question was asked: If low-cost goods were to be brought into Mexico from an even lower cost nation and assembled, could these goods then be imported into the United States duty free or at a significantly reduced duty? The negotiators worked hard at devising solutions to this problem. Nearly 200 pages were devoted to this topic alone. The result was to promote NAFTA originated components for use in any goods in intra-NAFTA trade. When this is not possible, exceptions are made.

Certificates of origin are required by exporters and must be kept on file by importers if goods are declared subject to the preferential tariff provisions of NAFTA. If the goods are not subject to tariff, it is not necessary to get a certificate of origin. If the goods are totally sourced in a NAFTA country, such as an agricultural product or coal, there is no difficulty in proving its NAFTA eligibility. If the good is made up of a number of components, it is necessary to trace the origin of each of the components. This is a further clarification of the FTA rules because of a conflict over Honda automobiles assembled in Canada with a motor that was "manufactured" in Ohio before the car was imported to the United States. The U.S. customs official valued each of the components and declared that the automobile was ineligible for FTA benefits. To prevent such confusion, the rules of origin of NAFTA have been spelled out, but they are very complicated nonetheless.

If a good imported into one of the member nations under one tariff classification of the Harmonized System of Tariffs is transformed through a degree of processing or manufacturing, then that good is subject to a different classification number and becomes NAFTA eligible. If, however, there is not a "substantial transformation," then the "net cost" or "regional value" must be considered in order to make the determination. The net cost is determined by the total cost of producing the goods, deducting the costs of sales promotion, marketing and after-sales services, packing, and shipping. In most cases, if 50 percent of the net cost or 60 percent of value of the good is of regional content, then the good is eligible for NAFTA treatment. If goods traded among the three nations do not qualify for NAFTA treatment, they must be given the same preferential treatment accorded other nations under the "most favored nation" provisions of its Treaties of Friendship and Commerce.

Certain sectors—automotive, textile and apparel, energy and basic petrochemicals and agriculture—also were given special treatment under the provisions of Part II: Trade in Goods.

Automobiles. These were covered under the most stringent rules of origin, requiring that 62.5 percent of the value must be of regional origin and 60 percent of the value of automobile parts. Determination of value for automobiles included the "net cost" of all components, based on the Honda example and the FTA. Mexico should phase out 36 percent local content over ten years. Mexican tariffs on automobiles and light trucks were reduced by 50 percent as of January 1, 1994. Tariffs on automobiles would decrease at the 10 percent rate, while those for trucks would decrease 20 percent annually. A significant increase in exports of U.S. manufactured cars and trucks is estimated, as a Mexican manufactured car costs $600 more than its equivalent manufactured in Detroit.

Textile and Apparel. This is one of the most internationally protected sectors, and it was a sensitive area for negotiators. Mexico agreed to decrease its tariff 50 percent immediately, with the remainder over five years, on imported textiles and fabrics. The United States placed textiles on a ten-year phase-in reduction for the quotas that were in place. Here, too, there was concern about the use of non-regional raw materials in textiles and apparel. A "yarn forward" rule of origin applies to finished goods that are composed of fabric formed in North America with yarn made in North America to be eligible for reduced duty treatment. An exception to the "yarn forward" rule is the "fiber forward" rule. Any apparel that is produced from fibers that are in short supply in North America are "fiber forward." These include silk and linen apparel, fine cotton products, women's underwear, etc.

Energy and Petrochemicals. Mexico retained protection of basic oil and natural gas exploration, exploitation, and selling; however, the United States persuaded Mexico to permit U.S. and Canadian oil field service companies to participate with PEMEX, the state-owned oil company. Their participation will not, however, permit them to have a percentage of ownership, which is frequently the case in these arrangements. Investment will be permitted in the majority of petrochemical sectors. For natural gas, U.S. and Canadian marketers will negotiate supply agreements directly with the suppliers and end-users in Mexico, but still are limited to using PEMEX's facilities. Electrical power now may be generated by independent companies, and the surplus, or co-generation, must be sold to the Mexican electric company, CFE, at prices to be determined by CFE. Canada did not protect the energy sector under the FTA, and did not prevent U.S. investment. Canada is committed to providing the U.S. with energy in the case of emergency, a provision that was not imposed on Mexico.

Agriculture. There are three bilateral agreements: one between the U.S and Canada negotiated under FTA, and those between the U.S. and Mexico, and Mexico and Canada. The U.S. persuaded Mexico to engage in "tariffication" of Mexican non-tariff barriers, i.e., import licensing. Tariffs on agricultural goods, comprising 50 percent of southern border trade, will be eliminated immediately, followed by additional tariffs within five years. Sensitive products in Mexico (corn, dairy products, and edible beans), in the U.S. (orange juice concentrate, sugar, broccoli, asparagus, onions, and cauliflower), and in Canada (eggs, dairy, sugar, and poultry) all will have the 15-year phase-out.

Government Procurement

NAFTA increases the type of government agencies that are subject to procurement bidding and also extends the coverage to trade in services, i.e., construction contracts. Federal government procurement is available in all three nations, and U.S. and Canadian companies can bid on 50 percent of PEMEX and CFE goods and service contracts. This 50 percent also will be reduced over ten years. All nationals of the North American region shall be treated as if they were nationals of that particular government for procurement purposes. There are thresholds below which foreigners are not eligible to bid: $50,000 for government entities for goods and/or services, and $6.5 million for construction services. The minimums for government enterprises are $250,000 and $8 million, respectively. Programs that are in place to promote "buying" national goods are to be phased out in all three nations.

Investment, Services, and Related Matters

Here again NAFTA moves beyond existing trade agreements, including the FTA, by providing that all future services will be included automatically. It provides the protection of the FTA to guarantee providers of services with national treatment under any new laws and regulations the right to invest in certain service sectors, the right to sell services across the border, the right of professionals to cross the border under simplified visa conditions, and the right to public access to information on any law or regulation impacting them. In addition, telecommunications, financial services, and land transport are specifically included. Maritime transportation, civil aviation, broadcasting, and basic telephone services are specifically excluded.

Financial Services. For the first time in decades, Mexico has opened her financial sector to foreign investment. This sector includes banking, insurance, securities, and other non-banking services. Each of the nations retains its own regulatory program, and treats member nations as it would its own nationals. It will be 13 years before Mexican banking and securities are completely open, whereas, it will be six years minimum for insurance and other non-banking services. Cross-border trade in services also is to be permitted. Provisions for dispute resolution by financial experts, procedural transparency, and the right of establishment all are guaranteed.

Telecommunications. All three nations reserve the right to exempt basic telephone service, but for what are referred to as "enhanced services," each nation has promised to provide equal opportunity to companies of the other signatory nations to participate on a non-discriminatory basis. To make this a reality, each nation has pledged to abide by agreed-upon technical standards and make all rules and regulations governing the provision of such services readily available.

Land Transportation. NAFTA eliminates the necessity of switching cargo to Mexican truck or driver at the border. Trucks may carry international cargo into the border states as of January 1, 1995, and throughout Mexico by January 1, 2000. These provisions, of course, also are available to Mexican carriers in the United States and Canada. Mexican trucks and truck drivers will have to meet U.S. safety standards. In addition, the requirements will be harmonized among the three nations within three years. U.S. and Canadian companies can invest in Mexican carriers who provide international transport. For an indefinite period, Mexico has reserved domestic land transport solely for Mexican nationals. U.S. and Canadian investors will be able to build and own railroads and terminals, but will be required to employ Mexican crews.

Investment. NAFTA will guarantee the continuance of Mexico's present investment reforms. The U.S. and Mexico will treat all citizens and corporations incorporated in each other's territory as nationals, regardless of who owns the corporation. Canada will consider who owns the corporation to determine whether it is eligible for NAFTA treatment. Screening of investments is permitted. Mexico can review any investment over $25 million, the United States can continue to apply "Exon-Florio" tests if there is a question of national security, and the Canadians will retain the FTA review process. National treatment for investors occurs unless there are circumstances in which "most favored nation" status would be more beneficial. Free convertibility of currency also is guaranteed, although some sectors may be restricted.

Temporary Entry for Business Persons. Before NAFTA, Mexicans were not eligible for certain U.S. non-immigrant visas, such as treaty investor or treaty trade (the so-called "E" visas). Now, an additional 5,000 Mexicans will be eligible to enter the United States as professionals for one year to work for U.S. companies. This provision had been included in the Canada–U.S. Free Trade Agreement without limitation as to numbers. The restriction is to be reviewed after several years.

Intellectual Property

This is the first trade agreement that includes intellectual property. Mexico has guaranteed to uphold the international conventions on intellectual property, and the protection accorded patents, trademarks, copyrights, and trade secrets under Mexican law are extended.

Dispute Mechanisms

NAFTA, along the lines of the Canada–U.S. Free Trade Agreement, establishes tri-national panels to review disputes rather than use the courts of each jurisdiction. It is a multi-step process beginning with consultation. The Agreement also recommends that commercial disputes between business people be settled through arbitration and conciliation rather than through litigation.

In addition, and as a result of the side agreements negotiated by the Clinton administration, provisions were made for protection of labor and clearer provisions established for the protection of the environment.

Labor. Because the side agreements did not provide for independent unions or collective bargaining, U.S. labor unions were dissatisfied with the extent to which labor was protected. This is the first trade agreement that has specifically addressed the workplace.

Environmental Protection. Canada, Mexico, and the U.S. will uphold existing rules and regulations protecting the environment. Furthermore, all three nations will permit tightening of regulations, provided they are not discriminatory. Strict environmental laws in states and cities, possibly more strict than federal governments, will not violate NAFTA. A trilateral commission will establish minimum standards for environmental matters and also be empowered to conduct investigations as to alleged violations. If violations are found again after a multi-tiered investigation and hearing process, the U.S. and Mexico agree to be subject to sanctions; Canada insists on having the matter enforced by Canadian courts.

Opportunities and Challenges

The North American Free Trade Agreement presents the three signatory nations with great opportunities for creating an integrated economic system in which the comparative advantages of each are given full opportunity to develop within a larger trading bloc than had previously existed. At the same time, these opportunities can create problems as adjustment is made to the new system.

The negotiators of the Agreement were cognizant of the potential downside of the Agreement. As a result, provisions were made to exclude certain sectors that were politically too sensitive, such as primary energy in Mexico and "cultural industries" in Canada. The staggered tariff reductions were intended to provide sufficient time for businesses and sectors to make those changes necessary to maintain their viability in the new trade area.

In the United States, the Bush and Clinton administrations promised federal funds would be available for those dislocated as a result of changes. Whereas the Bush administration did not link such dislocation allowances and retraining directly to NAFTA losses, the Clinton proposal does incorporate federal funding for programs tied to NAFTA losses. Substantially less funds are being made available to the program, which may be a direct result of the narrowing of the benefit.

Labor unions fear that jobs will migrate from the north to Mexico, a fear shared by both Canadian and U.S. union leadership. The issue in the United States has been complicated by the increasing unemployment of the less-well-educated, which requires job retraining with or without NAFTA. Clearly, if the United States is to retain a competitive edge, it must have a work force that is sufficiently trained to perform high value-added skills to justify the higher wages paid. This job retraining is indeed a challenge.

Many opportunities exist. Whereas the United States is a mature economy, Mexico is one that is still growing. Many sectors in both the commercial and consumer markets will be expanding for decades to come. Sectors that were previously closed, such as government procurement at the federal level, will also expand. Infrastructure needs in Mexico have been recognized, and the government is seeking to improve the roads, the telecommunications grid, the housing base, etc., to promote the well-being of the Mexican people. Investment opportunities have been created in previously unavailable sectors, such as financial services, including banking, insurance, and brokerage. Here again, the Mexican market is underserved in the number of institutions and their products, creating enormous opportunities for those who can provide alternatives.

In turn, there are sectors in which the Mexican producer may well provide products that can create dislocations in the U.S. economy. The agricultural sector feared increased imports of sugar and citrus in amounts that would devastate existing growers. As a result, special provisions were negotiated after both the Agreement and the side agreements had been negotiated to gain passage in the United States. The Mexicans are aware that the lack of modernity and efficiency will cause great dislocation in their agricultural sector, i.e., from the grain producers, but did not make such protection, beyond the previously negotiated "snapback" provisions and the negotiations for the side agreement on Import Surges, part of their demands.

U.S. and Canadian companies that are willing to accept the challenge of entering the Mexican market will be rewarded if, and only if, they do their homework in advance. It is not sufficient just to determine that there is a market niche and develop an understanding of the legal and regulatory climate. Companies must also be aware of the cultural and social requirements of Mexico.

Summary

Despite the debate over entering into the North American Free Trade Agreement, the Conference Board survey of 1,250 manufacturers demonstrated that "sustained growth and profitability depend on active and broad-based international operations" [5]. The study found that corporations with global activities grew faster and in every size category than those without global activities. The challenge and the opportunities of NAFTA are significant. It remains for the Canadians, Americans, and Mexicans to work together over the long term as partners for the their mutual benefit.

References

1. Szule, T., "Don't Take Canada for Granted," *Parade Magazine,* February 20, 1994.
2. *New York Times,* February 15, 1977.

3. Mills, J., "Business Lobbying for Trade Pact Appears to Sway Few in Congress," *New York Times,* November 12, 1993.
4. "Across the Rio Grande," *The Economist,* October 9, 1993.
5. Taylor, C. and G. Foster, "The Necessity of Being Global," *Across the Board* (Conference Board Publication), February 1994.

Historical Context for the NAFTA Challenge

The NAFTA community composed of three distinct nations, each with its own colorful history and sense of identity, was created for commercial reasons. The commercial fates of three diverse peoples have been united. This event presages an even greater degree of intercultural interaction between coming generations of Americans, Canadians, and Mexicans. Economic necessity brought these three nations together, and the potential for enhanced economic advantage in the world economy has given voice to countless overtures of cooperation. Yet each of the countries now, perhaps as much as at any other time in their histories, continues to wrestle with forces that call into question their own historical identities as they are swept by the internal and external forces of change.

Americans, Canadians, and Mexicans continue to harbor many misconceptions as a result of simple ignorance or perhaps of conscious efforts to justify or rationalize national ideologies. NAFTA is recognition of an increasingly obvious economic and cultural integration between three neighboring countries.

In this chapter we will look briefly at some of the major diplomatic, historical and social interactions between each of the three countries as illustrated in their attitudes and histories.

NAFTA and the United States' Concept of Manifest Destiny

Canada and Mexico share many common experiences in their historical relationship to the United States, including economic and cultural penetration and loss of territory. As early as the presidency of Thomas Jefferson, Americans dreamed of the extension of their "chosen" way of life to the Mississippi, and within a few short years, with the settlement of this area, their sights shifted to envision an America that stretched "from sea to shining sea."

Manifest Destiny is the philosophy that led Americans to believe that North America would eventually be composed of states that would willingly choose the American model. Therefore, when Americans crossed into the territory of other nations as settlers, they felt a right to establish a compact with the land, believing it was the American way to prosper by extending American boundaries.

Thus, while Mexicans will never forget, nor likely forgive, the conquest of half of their country in 1847, Americans give little thought to the matter. For them it was an inevitable occurrence. Generally, Americans are defensive about this aspect of their national history.

Americans should be aware that while there are attractive features of their country, the same is true of every country. Despite the fact "Canada and Mexico both have highly asymmetrical relationships with their common neighbor, which is more truly dependence in the case of Mexico" [1], NAFTA does not mean that Canada and Mexico will become or should want to become commercial annexes of the United States.

Canada and the United States—Colonial Origins

The historical relationship between Canada and the United States is reflected in a recent statement by Prime Minister Jean Chrétien, a statement that could as easily have been made 200 years ago as today. "The United States is so big that if we don't look independent, you Americans will take us for granted," said Chrétien. "We like each other, I just don't want Canada to be perceived as the 51st state of America. Because we're not America—we're Canada" [2].

Many of the feelings that exist between Canadians and Americans today have been present since the earliest colonial times. Generally speaking, the French fur traders, or *coureurs de bois,* settled the continent's interior, while the English colonists hugged the coastline. In the 1763 Treaty of Paris, which helped shape the future of North America, the French gave up their claims to empire in the new world, leaving the English in possession of what was then a largely French-speaking Canada.

"The French Colony in Canada, not yet to be called a nation, survived as a French and a Catholic community" [3]. The English, extraordinarily liberal for the times, allowed Quebec to survive as a cultural island. Under the Quebec Act of 1774, religious toleration was guaranteed, permitting Catholics to hold government office, and Quebec's traditions of French civil law and its *seigneurial* system of rural land distribution to survive intact. Although many French Canadians left Quebec to seek their fortunes in New England, this act shaped Canada's modern-day bicultural identity.

Revolution and Evolution

In 1776, the United States drafted a daring Declaration of Independence and began a long war for independence. In 1789 it ratified a newly created Constitution. Canada, loyal to the British Crown and well-satisfied by the protection afforded to citizens by the British Parliament, proudly remained a colony, while its neighbor underwent this process of rebirth and self-baptism. Thus, while the United States had its fiercely original defining moments, Canada chose to evolve peacefully within the British Empire. To prevent further problems in the colonies, Britain gave Canada many of the concessions that it had given to the newly independent United States, "so Canada never had to fight to end taxation without representation. The Americans had won that battle for them" [4].

As a result of its revolutionary origins, and no doubt reinforced by its success, a messianic element is part of the American world view. This view can result in a sort of prescriptive and missionary belief in U.S.-style democracy and the "American way." What to Americans are good intentions emanating from a sincere and unquestioning belief in the functional and moral superiority of their values and systems, often appears to their alleged beneficiaries as preponderant interventionism at best or, at worst, the unabashed pursuit of self interest. A difference of opinion about U.S. intentions always has existed between the United States and Canada. A fundamental part of this difference can be explained, perhaps, by the difference between revolution and evolution, and the role that each respective process plays in the development of a national identity.

A distinctive feature throughout Canada's existence is the search for a national identity that is meaningfully different from that of the United States. Although every Canadian knows there are differences, and a visitor to Canada can feel them, they are hard to enumerate. This is the burden of a small country occupying a vast territory adjacent to a powerful and culturally similar neighbor.

War of 1812

In 1812, the United States attacked Britain in defense of its maritime rights. At the 1818 peace conference, the 49th parallel was adopted as the American-Canadian border, and the continent was effectively divided by what remains the world's longest peaceful and unarmed border. The peace treaty, along with the Monroe Doctrine, clearly expressed that supremacy in North America reposed with the United States. The power of imperial Great Britain counterbalanced any intentions the U.S. might have had to invade Canada in the 1800s, and Canada always had British influence to counterbalance the economic pull of the U.S.

Manifest Destiny and Border Disputes

Canada's mistrust of American intentions is not altogether unfounded historically. During the 1800s, numerous border disputes took place between the two countries. At the time, however, Canada was still represented by Britain in matters of foreign policy. Britain had its own interests to protect, and on several occasions used Canadian territory to appease America.

Border disputes in Maine, concluding in 1842 with the Webster-Ashburton Treaty, awarded seven-twelfths of the disputed territory to the United States. A favorable decision in relation to the border between Oregon and British Columbia gave the United States a more desirable access to Puget Sound, as well.

In 1903, the Alaskan border dispute also was resolved in favor of the Americans by an arbitration board composed of three Americans, two Canadians, and an Englishman. The Americans, Teddy Roosevelt's personal cronies, were seen by Canadians as anything but impartial. Canadians felt they had been duped by Roosevelt, who additionally threatened to run troops along the border to ensure the favorable resolution of the question. To make matters worse, the British member of the arbitration board voted against Canada to court American friendship in what was becoming for them a naval arms race against the Germans.

The American Civil War and
The British North America Act

During the American Civil War, Great Britain allowed the Confederacy to construct and repair ships in its shipyards, which enraged a great many Americans. Anti-British sentiments were high, while at the same time controversy over fishing rights off the coast of Newfoundland and disputes over the United States border with British Columbia in the Puget Sound arose.

At this time, many leaders in Canada felt that some form of unification would be the only way to avoid annexation by the United States. Therefore, "on July 1, 1867, Canada East, Canada West, Nova Scotia, and New Brunswick joined together under the terms of the British North America Act to become the Dominion of Canada. The government of the new country was based upon the parliamentary system, with a governor general (the Crown's representative) and a Parliament consisting of the House of Commons and the Senate"[5]. As a confederation, Canada hoped to resist the gravitational pull of the United States.

Concurrent with the weakening of the British Empire, and in recognition of the large and independent role it played in World War I and in the dysfunctional League of Nations, Canada became an independent nation and "gained virtually complete constitutional autonomy" with the passage of the

Statute of Westminster in 1931 [6]. It was not until 1982, however, that the British North America Act was repatriated from the British Parliament in Westminster and brought home to Ottawa, where it was renamed the Constitution Act on April 17, 1982. Thus, the process of Canadian governmental evolution lasted almost as long as the entire history of the country.

Cultural Influence

Out of a traditional geographic necessity, much of Canada's population lives along a narrow stretch of land that hugs and parallels the American border, making it more susceptible to inadvertent American cultural penetration.

To counter American cultural penetration, or perhaps better said, to encourage a resurgence of genuine Canadian culture, the Canadian government enacted a series of successful laws and programs in the late 1960s that were designed to protect its cultural industries and support Canadian producers of cultural material. Due to the success of such programs, Canadian sensitivity to this matter, while still present, has declined.

Someone once said "the more things change, the more they stay the same." That is certainly true with respect to U.S.-Canadian relations. Many of the issues that today divide and sensitize Canadian-U.S. relations have been present since the earliest colonial times and throughout the two nations' histories. Thankfully, the great and historic synergy these two proud countries share has been recognized under NAFTA, and an even more promising future can be built upon the past achievements of hard work, friendship, and mutual respect.

Canada and Mexico[1]

Obviously, given that Canada and Mexico are separated by the United States, the nature of their contact has been much less profound than either of the two countries' respective interactions with

---

[1] Much of the information for this section is based upon comments from a speech given by J. Ian Burchett, Canadian Consul & Trade Commissioner in Monterrey, Mexico.

the U.S. However, it is worthwhile to note that this geographical separation is nothing with which Mexicans and Canadians are unfamiliar, for both of their countries are enormous.

A recent advertisement from The Bank of Montreal said it all:

> Canada and Mexico share a continent, but they have long been strangers to each other. Both have been intent upon the internal development of their vast territories and abundant resources. And perhaps neither has been able to see past the overwhelming presence of the United States and recognize a neighbor on the other side. Yet for both Mexico and Canada, the other country is a new frontier with virtually limitless economic potential [7].

Canadian business visitors to Mexico not only go away with impressions of beautiful beaches and archaeological ruins, but also modern manufacturing facilities, bustling cities, power lunches, and cellular telephones. Few Canadians or Mexicans are aware, however, that the business relationship the two countries share goes back to the last century, when the first Canadian business mission arrived in the 1850s [8].

Despite whatever growth in understanding and strengthening of ties needs to take place between Canada and Mexico, there is indeed a history of interactions between the two countries. Before the end of the previous century, for example, Canadians founded Mexico Light and Power, a company that eventually constructed the electric power plants and streetcar systems in Mexico City and Monterrey.

Lago Toronto and Lago Winnipeg, two reservoirs dug by Canadians in the 1920s in the northern state of Chihuahua, still play a crucial role in important agricultural irrigation systems in that state. Over 50,000 Mennonites of Canadian descent reside in that state as well, bringing a stoic Canadian protestantism with them that contributes to Mexico's cultural diversity.

In 1944, just before the GATT came into existence, Mexico and Canada signed their first reciprocal trade agreement. Once GATT was implemented, Mexico was granted "Most Favored Nation" status, which was upgraded to even more preferential treatment in 1974. As the foundation of a strengthened bilateral trade relationship to which both were committed, Canadian Prime Minister Mulroney and Mexican President Carlos Salinas de Gortari signed an agreement on Trade and Economic Cooperation in 1990.

In 1993, trade between Mexico and Canada exceeded $2 billion, and could potentially double within five years. Mexico is already Canada's most important trading partner in Latin America, and its fifth largest supplier overall, behind the United States, Japan, the United Kingdom, and Germany.

Canada, correspondingly, is Mexico's sixth largest source of imports. In 1993, there were more than 300 Canadian "fixed investments" in Mexico. All such statistics must be viewed skeptically, however, because the United States is a major obstacle to the accurate valuation of Canada-Mexico trade.

For example, while countless truck loads of auto parts, computer and electronic components, and telecommunications equipment ultimately arrive in Monterrey and Guadalajara, they are accounted for as exports destined for the United States because they are first sent to an intermediate destination in the United States. As such, some credible sources have speculated that Canada-Mexico trade could be undervalued by as much as 50 percent [9].

Both governments realized during the NAFTA negotiations that they had a lot in common, in terms of values, aspirations, and concerns—especially those in relation to the United States. The NAFTA negotiations brought the two countries closer together than ever, and in 1994 they will celebrate the 50th anniversary of their bilateral trade relationship.

The governments and private sectors in both countries are working hard to design strategies for different products in certain markets, hoping to build upon the strength and experience of local partners familiar with the region and desirous of a long-term partnership. For Canada, like Mexico, the key words are joint venturing and strategic partnering, competitive and flexible financing, and business leadership in targeted market niche segments [10].

Canada and Mexico lack as extensive an historical interaction as each has had separately with the United States. Both countries do have an extremely positive relationship, and one which is of growing significance to both. They now have the opportunity to take advantage of the historic challenge that NAFTA poses for them by continuing to develop business associations that create synergies based on current experiences between their cultures, technologies, and competitive factors of production.

Mexico and the United States

Of the three countries involved in NAFTA, the two that will have the hardest time overcoming the scars of history are Mexico and the United States. Indeed, NAFTA is one of the only truly positive interactions the countries have had since 1821, when Mexico achieved its independence from Spain.

The American Annexation of Texas

After achieving independence in 1821, Mexico experienced a period of extreme political chaos and economic weakness, during which more than 50 different presidents took office in as many years. During this time, American Manifest Destiny was in full force and settlers were streaming westward, some of them arriving in what is now Texas.

Many Americans believed that Texas to the Rio Grande River had been part of Thomas Jefferson's Louisiana Purchase. Mexicans knew the territory to be a part of the state of Coahuila. Nonetheless, over 20,000 American settlers began to arrive in the territory by the year 1830. As they were in Mexico, the settlers were expected to obey Mexican laws, requiring that they be Catholic, pledge obedience to Mexico, and after 1830, that they not hold slaves.

Needless to say, they did not obey, and Mexico, frustrated at its inability to control the situation, prohibited further settlement after 1830. On several occasions, the U.S. offered to buy Texas to solve the problem—offers that met with indignant refusals by Mexico. The settlers, having come from other eastern areas of the United States, had different expectations about the type of government they desired, which did not mesh well with the small Mexican population whom they quickly outnumbered. The Americans felt that the Mexican system was inefficient, and that Mexicans were lazy or even inferior.

Believing in the American principle of self determination, the settlers felt it their right to elect to become a member state of the United States. In 1835, Texans began a war that ended in the 1836 defeat of Mexican General Santa Anna, who surrendered Texas. Due to indecision about whether it would be a slave or free state, Texas was not officially annexed by the United States until 1845, which immediately prompted a break in diplomatic relations with Mexico.

The War of The North American Invasion and Gadsen Purchase

According to historian Stanley R. Ross, Mexicans perceive their relationship with the United States as one shaped by "armed conflict, military invasion, and economic and cultural penetration" [11]. The military invasion began with a war that Mexicans call the "War of the North American Invasion," an event that many future-oriented Americans are not aware ever occurred, and which Mexico's intense preoccupation with the past can never allow it to forget. American business people are advised to be aware of this event, and sensitive to the importance it continues to hold for Mexicans. Mexicans ought not blame current generations of Americans for it.

When, in 1845, a dispute arose over where the southern border of the newly formed state of Texas would be placed—at the Nueces River (Mexican claim) or at the Rio Grande River (American claim)—President Polk sent American troops to the area to "protect" the border. During the same time, Americans had entered California and New Mexico and were planning for the day when they, like Texas, would enter the union. Indeed, American army surveyors were already in California; Polk was openly interested in territorial expansion. He ordered U.S. troops to cross into the disputed area in Texas, and simultaneously sent a minister to Mexico to try to buy the Mexican territory. The offer was refused by the Mexicans, justifiably angered by the presence of U.S. forces in the areas under question. Polk tried to get Congress to declare war on Mexico, but it would not. War ultimately was declared when Mexican troops attacked a U.S. unit in the disputed territory, and it was claimed that Mexico had "shed U.S. blood on U.S. soil."

The basic U.S. goal in the war was to occupy the areas of Mexican territory that it wanted, and then force Mexico to surrender them. The city of Monterrey, today's free trade capital in

Mexico, was attacked and occupied, as were New Mexico and California. When Mexico refused to give up the occupied areas, U.S. troops entered at the port of Veracruz and advanced all the way to Mexico City, which they also occupied. In the Treaty of Guadalupe Hidalgo, all American claims were granted, and the United States agreed to pay Mexico $15 million for the territory. There was considerable talk in the American press, and even from President Polk, of the possibility of annexing all of Mexico.

Several years after the end of the war, in what was called the Gadsden Purchase, additional Mexican lands in Arizona and New Mexico were purchased from a Mexico that was in no position to decline the offer. Overnight, Mexicans became minorities in new Anglo-American states. Discrimination against the native Mexican populations remaining in the newly acquired territories served the interest of the new settlers who would take their land and disenfranchise them from participating in what had been their society.

> The victory of the Anglos was quick and cruel. . . . The Mexicans lost their lands, their language and their culture. . . . The extent to which racism was employed in the cultural and economic conquest of California is exemplified by the Greaser law, an anti-vagrancy statute passed in 1856, which actually referred to people 'known as greasers.' Such wars leave scars that cannot be overcome. Racism is compounded by history and the economics of land forever lost. Rage ebbs into nostalgia and regret. The bitter taste of 1848 affects all intercourse between Mexicans and Anglos, and it lives in every encounter between Mexicans and U.S. descendants of Mexicans [12].

U.S. Commercial Involvement During the "Porfiriato"

During the period from 1870 to 1910, known by Mexicans as the *porfiriato* for the rule of the dictatorial Porfirio Diaz, Mexico enjoyed its first period of political stability, as well as substantial industrialization and economic growth. By 1910, the U.S. bought three quarters of Mexican exports, and was the major source of the foreign investment which had accelerated the economic progress in the country [13]. "They owned over half the oil, two-thirds of the railroads, and three-fourths of the mines and smelters" [14]. Americans were very pleased by the profits they made in Mexico and by the stability Diaz provided during his rule, but little economic or social benefit accrued to the Mexican population, who overthrew him in 1910.

U.S. Intervention During and After the Mexican Revolution

Porfirio Diaz was overthrown in 1910 by the reformer Francisco I. Madero. In a plot involving the U.S. ambassador, Madero was murdered and replaced by Victoriano Huerta shortly before Woodrow Wilson was elected president of the United States. U.S. business interests welcomed the authoritarian Huerta as a return to stable profits, but President Wilson, interfering on the first of many occasions in Mexican affairs, refused to recognize Huerta's government in hopes of influencing revolution in Mexico towards a constitutional democracy.

Huerta continued to consolidate his hold on Mexico, and Wilson became increasingly impatient, offering to send U.S. troops to the aid of Huerta's opponent Venustiano Carranza. Carranza refused his offer. The arrest of several off-duty and unruly U.S. marines in Veracruz precipitated the dispatch of a large American naval presence to the area. Presumably to stop a shipload of German arms from reaching Huerta, Wilson ordered the seizure of the Port of Veracruz in 1914, with considerable violence and loss of life on both sides.

During the negotiations between the representatives of Wilson and Huerta following the Veracruz incident, Carranza forced Huerta out of power. Shortly thereafter, Carranza was betrayed by one of his generals, Francisco "Pancho" Villa, and civil war raged again in Mexico.

When the Carranza government was given de facto recognition by the United States, Villa became enraged, killed 16 Americans, and later invaded the town of Columbus, New Mexico. A punitive expedition, ordered by Wilson, was initiated, resulting in American troops being present in Mexico again during the period of March 1916 to March 1917. President Carranza issued what came to be known as the Carranza Doctrine against foreign intervention in Mexico.

With the start of World War I, the Carranza government was officially recognized, but America continued to apply pressure regarding certain elements of the new Mexican Constitution, specifically Article 27. Article 27 established the state's ultimate authority over soil and subsoil rights. This meant that the government could interfere in the oil and mining industries, which were largely under American control.

The bilateral agenda continued to focus on issues surrounding foreign investment, especially those related to petroleum, during the 1920s and 1930s. Under pressure from U.S. business interests, President Harding withdrew diplomatic recognition of the Mexican government until he received a promise that Mexico would not seize or interfere in any oil operations that had existed prior to 1917.

Nationalization of Petroleum and Banking and 1982 Debt Crisis

Despite significant efforts by the U.S., in 1938, under the power contained within Article 27 of the Mexican Constitution and in the name of protecting and preserving the national patrimony, all foreign oil companies were nationalized. The state-owned Mexican oil company PEMEX was created.

During the 1980s, Mexican banks were nationalized. Although they have since been reprivatized, a great uneasiness was created about the safety of investments in Mexico. Many investors rightfully wondered if Mexico really was reforming, or if it would again suddenly reverse its current policies and confiscate foreign assets and investment.

In 1982, Mexico suffered a crippling debt crisis. Although its debts with American commercial banks were successfully renegotiated under the Brady Plan, Mexico's international reputation was severely discredited. Another long held stereotype of Mexicans, that of their laziness, was reinforced. Americans always have noted what they considered a latin economic inferiority, and supposedly Mexico again was providing evidence of this.

In the "Protestant work ethic," as articulated by the German Max Weber, virtue in people is seen through their actions and their work. Americans and Canadians are seen by Mexicans as living to work and as overly materialistic. This work-oriented behavior is the source of Canadian and American pride and self-respect. Long-held Canadian and American stereotypes about Mexicans regard them as lazy, untrustworthy, and lacking in the gauge of what is important to those with a work ethic: material development.

NAFTA's Historic Challenge

Nations traditionally have been organized based upon the supposition that they are serving the collective needs of their population. When the needs and aspirations of nations come into conflict, so do the sentiments of their population. History has time and again confirmed this causality.

Mexicans and Canadians may feel that, in many ways, they have been treated insensitively or as less than equals by the United States throughout history. Americans may believe in the defensibility of what they have done. This is in no way an attempt to judge whether such feelings are right or wrong, or whether Canada, the United States, or Mexico is good or bad.

The historic challenge faced by the citizens of three great and unique nations is to evaluate business relationships and actions with citizens from the other signatory countries based upon the present—their present. Successful international managers strive to conduct business relationships in the present, evaluating one another regardless of culture or nationality as individuals, based upon personal and direct experiences, rather than the historical, impersonal, and stereotypical expectations history has instilled.

NAFTA was negotiated by representatives of all three countries who were cognizant of the needs, priorities, and potentials of their nations. For NAFTA to work, we must place trust in its history, one that it is up to us to form. With the rules of the game redefined, if we can imagine it, we can play increasingly on the same team, creating a synergy of our historical strengths and national characters and cultures that enriches the entire NAFTA region both culturally and economically.

To begin to create new history under NAFTA, rich with the rewards of profitable and culturally sensitive relationships, we must understand our respective histories more clearly so that we can overcome the temptation to let impersonal experience and national legends guide our personal and business interactions.

References

1. "Canadian and Mexican Trade Policies Towards the United States: A Perspective From Canada," *Canada and International Trade*, The Institute of Public Policy, 1985, p. 11.
2. Szulc, T., "Don't Take Canada for Granted," *Parade Magazine*, February 20, 1994, p. 4.
3. Morton, W.L., *The Canadian Identity*, Toronto: University of Toronto, 1972, p. 14.
4. Ibid.
5. "Facts Canada—History," Foreign Affairs and International Trade Canada, number 8, 1993.
6. "Facts Canada," Foreign Affairs and International Trade Canada, number 9, 1993.
7. Fedorowicz, J., *Mexico-Canada: Partnering for Success*, Ontario: Prospectus Publications Ltd., 1992, p. 12.
8. Comments excerpted from a speech given by J. Ian Burchett, Canadian Consul and Trade Commissioner in Monterrey, Mexico.
9. Fedorowicz, J., *Mexico-Canada: Partnering for Success*, Ontario: Prospectus Publications Ltd., 1992, p. 43.
10. Comments excerpted from a speech given by J. Ian Burchett, Canadian Consul and Trade Commissioner in Monterrey, Mexico.
11. Ross, S.R. and R. Erb, "Mexican-U.S. Relations: An Historical Perspective," *U.S. Policies Toward Mexico: Perceptions and Perspectives*, American Institute for Public Policy Research, 1979, p. 9.
12. Shorris, E., *Latinos A Biography of the People*, New York: W.W. Norton and Co., 1992, pp. 31–32 and 39.

13. *El Desafío de la Interdependencia: México y Estados Unidos,* Informe de la Comisión Sobre el Futuro de las Relaciones Mexico-Estados Unidos, 1988, p. 23.

14. Current, R.N., Williams, T.H. and Freidel, F., *American History: A Survey,* New York: Alfred A. Knopf, 1979, p. 593.

Understanding NAFTA's Cultures and Cultural Values

Within the widely diverse region that is North America are three nations, each of which has a distinct national culture enriched by innumerable subcultures. Canada, Mexico, and the United States each have a strong national character, yet as NAFTA grows and takes shape and cross-border cultural diffusion continues to occur, an increasingly regional identity is developing in North America, if not in the minds of North Americans.

Canada, Mexico, and the United States share the historical legacy of the New World, and each has been richly endowed by nature with space and an abundance of resources that gives its people, from wherever they may come, an openness and friendliness that has been noted by many an international observer, if not always by one another.

"For better or for worse, in North America, however, the answer to the question 'where are you from?' transmits a great deal of information, not all of it accurate. 'Where you're from' is taken as a good indicator of 'where you're coming from'" [1], which is in large part determined by culture.

Culture

Culture is a phenomenon that grows with people, and which, like knowledge and technology, accumulates and changes throughout time. It is the unique response by a group of people to the physical and human environment confronting them in a particular location, and the survival mechanisms that they collectively develop and pass on consciously and unconsciously to succeeding generations.

Whether we are aware or unaware, culture aids us in making many of the daily decisions that we are forced to make. Culture is "a problem solving tool" [2]. It is "everything we think, do, and have" [3] as members of our society: attitudes, values, beliefs, faiths, traditions, habits, and customs, as well as our national patrimony in the form of historical locations, architecture, and the influence of the very land itself upon our character and *Geist* as a people.

To successfully navigate between multiple cultures, a skill that is already being demanded of the globally competent NAFTA executive, one must have an understanding of his or her own culture. Cultural self-awareness is furthered by the eye-opening opportunity to experience firsthand another people's way of doing things, much as learning a second language provides one with new insights into his or her own native tongue.

While each culture has evolved uniquely, certain common elements can be found in almost all cultures. These features, called *cultural universals,* are elements present in every culture to a greater or lesser degree.

By using a systems approach in which these common elements are seen to be component parts of the overall culture, one will have the necessary tools to reorient oneself more easily in a new culture. Instead of succumbing to the natural tendency to focus on subjective cultural differences, a more fruitful approach begins with the identification of objective cultural similarities. In so doing, a parallel is established to our own culture, something we already know. By way of this relation between similar elements, the new culture, despite its differences from our own, is legitimized in its own right.

This approach was developed by early cultural anthropologists (like the character of "Indiana Jones" from the movie "Raiders of the Lost Ark"), who, via "participant observation" sought to integrate themselves as functioning members of primitive societies to more fully understand them. The following are examples of cultural universals:

Family Systems. In Mexico and Quebec, families tend to be larger and include a closer and more extended kinship network. The family is an important source of individual support and identity, and has tended in the cases of both these cultures to reduce the mobility of workers. For English-speaking Canadians and Americans, who tend to be more individualistic, the family is smaller, more nuclear, and plays a smaller role in individual decisions.

Educational Systems. The manner in which young people, new members of society, or displaced workers are provided with skills, knowledge, and values [4]. There are significant disparities in the levels of education obtained by Mexicans as compared to Americans and Canadians, and there is a need for further language and cultural training in all three countries.

Economic Systems. The manner in which a society is organized for the production of goods and services [5]. Canada and the United States have traditionally been in the forefront of free market trading nations, while the Mexican economy was closed and relied on import substitution policies. Under NAFTA, the unilateral economic reforms begun in Mexico during the de la Madrid administration and continued during the Salinas administration will be institutionalized, gradually opening Mexico's market to international competition.

Political Systems. The dominant means of governance for maintaining order and exercising power and authority [6]. The government in Canada, the United States, and Mexico are based upon a federal system. While transparent multi-party systems exist in the former two countries, Mexico is effectively a single party system, with the ruling PRI party having been in power over 63 years. While democratic political reform in Mexico is needed, it will occur at a gradual pace, assisted by the economic stability Mexico hopes to gain via NAFTA.

Religious Systems. The manner in which each culture inculcates belief in the supernatural, or provides for non-material motivation for life [7]. In each of the three NAFTA countries, there is an official separation of church and state. Mexico and Quebec are predominantly Roman Catholic, while the United States and English-speaking Canada are largely multi-denominational protestant. This system may provide a people with motivation to achieve, as did the protestant "Manifest Destiny" in the United States, or it may preserve the status quo, as did the Catholic Church in its efforts to promote cultural survival in Quebec for nearly 300 years, until the "Quiet Revolution" of the 1960s lessened its hold on society.

Association Systems. The way that social and professional groups are formed in society. Professional organizations, such as Rotary International, exist in all three countries, but personal relationships continue to be a major factor in doing business successfully in Mexico. Canadian and American societies are highly individualistic and don't place as much importance on group memberships as do the more collective Mexicans.

Health Systems. A culture's attempts to cure and prevent the spread of disease amongst its population, and to provide emergency care for accident or disaster victims [8]. Canada and Mexico both have comprehensive social medicine schemes, whereas the U.S. is currently embroiled in heated discussions about a major revision of its largely private system.

Recreational Systems. The way in which people interact socially and make use of their leisure time. Traditional sports, and national and regional dancing are examples.

Managers who employ awareness of their own cultures in adapting themselves to other cultures will have a powerful tool at their disposal, gaining the advantage that cultural sensitivity and empathy provide in intercultural activities. This alone, however, will not guarantee their success; managers from all three countries are confronted with overcoming stereotypes and prejudices infused in their cultures and which predispose them to ethnocentric interpretations of events and practices in other countries.

Ethnocentrism is the belief in the inherent superiority of one's own culture, and the tendency to evaluate contemptuously all foreign things and people from its biased vantage point. Ethnocentrism manifests itself as xenophobia, a strong dislike or distrust of foreigners, and the resulting attitudes can lead to discrimination against foreigners when at home and isolation when abroad.

Stereotypes

In his book *The Power of Myth,* Joseph Campbell said that "the only way that you can describe a human being truly is by describing his imperfections" [9]. It is natural for members of one culture to form exclusionary attitudes towards those of another, if such attitudes promote the success of the society or justify discriminatory behavior towards non-members.

Such attitudes, or stereotypes, often are not based on personal experience or observation, but rather on rumors, hearsay, incomplete and one-sided stories, and other types of non-empirical evidence. National stereotypes frequently are based on racism and prejudices, and have attained acceptance as a set of values, beliefs and attitudes forged through common experience [10].

There is a long and rather vicious history of stereotyping in North America, most notably between Mexicans and Anglo-Americans. Such stereotypes "rather than reflecting original responses to unique situations, have become part of day-in, day-out existence" and "rest on the distinction of what in the eyes of the would-be exploiters of other humans is the civilization of the former and the barbarism of the latter" [11].

Stereotyping has emanated not only from North America, but has been responded to vigorously by Mexico and Latin America. Indeed, by their stereotyping, Latin Americans have demonstrated that the "most prevalent form of racism in the world in recent decades has been anti-Americanism" [12].

Because stereotyping is habitual, and promotes a feeling of belonging within one's own society, it is a hard habit to break. Yet, given the particularly tumultuous past relationship of Mexico and the United States, one of the most important and relevant tasks each reader can undertake to make NAFTA a success is to commit him or herself to evaluating others on the basis of personal experience and concrete evidence.

Stereotyping predisposes individuals from different cultures to believe that they are fundamentally incompatible, and that simply is not true. Even if it were, NAFTA has made North Americans part of a common trading region; whether they are ready for the enormous intercultural challenge this implies or not, they will benefit from a culturally sensitive outlook and an honest effort to respect and understand the world from one another's respective vantage point.

To facilitate this process, Table 3-1 presents several historical stereotypes illustrative of the long-standing cultural walls between Mexicans and North Americans that prospective "InterNAFTA" managers will have to scale.

According to Joseph Campbell: "I think that what we're seeking is an experience of being alive, so that our experiences on the purely physical plane will have resonances within our inner being and reality, so that we actually feel the rapture of being alive. That's what its all finally about, and that's what these clues help us to find within ourselves" [13]. By overcoming stereotypes, managers potentially will be invited to look "inside" some of NAFTA's other exciting cultures, to resonate with those on the inside, and to share a life-enriching cultural experience by seeing the world from another angle.

International Customs Survey

One way of ensuring foreign business hosts that a manager is respectful of their country and free of stereotypes is to fit naturally and gracefully into that culture's system of interpersonal communication and protocol.

When moving between cultures, the globally-minded manager is ever cognizant of his/her responsibility to respect the subtle social protocol that exists within each culture. By keenly observing the conduct of his/her host, the NAFTA manager can pick up frequently repeated patterns of verbal and non-verbal communication.

(text continued on page 46)

Table 3-1
Historical Stereotypes

VALUE AFFECTED	MEXICAN VIEW OF N. AMERICA	MEXICAN VIEW OF SELF	N. AMERICAN VIEW OF MEXICAN	N. AMERICAN VIEW OF SELF
Self Control	Cold, insensitive, emotionless	Deal passively with stress, saying *ni modo* when something doesn't go to plan	Emotional, volatile, feminine, undisciplined	Rational, calm, masculine, deals actively with stress through discipline in life
Type of Civilization	Condescending, contradictory, not credible	Traditional; technically inferior, morally superior	Primitive, in need of instruction on "how to do things"	Advanced, responsible for showing others how to have democracy and free trade
Racial Attitude	Indiscriminate racism; can't distinguish high class Mexican from Indian	Social classes have subtle shades; whiter is better; the masses cannot be elevated anyway; North Americans should be able to distinguish between high and low classes and accept high as equals	Indigenous people are inferior; mestizos combine the worst features of both races; the treatment of the lower classes is unjust, therefore higher classes deserve no respect	Racially superior, culturally heterogeneous, but racially homogeneous, racial intermixing not acceptable

table continues

43

Table 3-1 (continued)

VALUE AFFECTED	MEXICAN VIEW OF N. AMERICA	MEXICAN VIEW OF SELF	N. AMERICAN VIEW OF MEXICAN	N. AMERICAN VIEW OF SELF
Honesty and trustworthiness (hi-low context)	Manipulative, tactless, have ulterior motives against Mexico; can't be trusted	More important to be nice than objective; O.K. to bend truth or retain info if people's feelings are preserved (high-context)	Dishonest, indirect, sneaky, not trustworthy	Honest, direct, principled, literal (low-context)
Character	Aggressive, at times brutal and abusive	Brave but overpowered, like *niños heroes*	Submissive, weak	Dominant, strong
Time Orientation	Obsessively future oriented, doesn't know how to relax, unrealistically believes time can be mastered	Lives in and enjoys present, respects past, awaits a future to be determined by God's will: *si Dios quiere*	Lives too much in present while dwelling on past, surrenders own will and ambition to chance, procrastinating	The present is the birthplace of the future; planning, action-oriented; "all the flowers of all the tomorrows are in the seeds we plant today"
Social Classes	Although morally corrupted, economically and per-haps racially superior	Exclusive, but more cultured & civilized at top levels; money not only determinant	Chaotic, inefficient, unjust; high classes lack character and low classes lack potential	Orderly, efficient, fair; upward mobility is possible to anyone who has money to enter

of status for *gente decente* (decent people)

			Passive Christianity	Active Christianity
Religion	Profess a false religion	Repository of higher moral values	Passive Christianity (Catholicism) God's faithful servant	Active Christianity (Protestantism) God's appointed steward
Orientation to Nature	Destructive, futilely trying to control what only God can master	Nature merely "is," a creation of God which man can ultimately neither influence nor control	Man cannot control nature; fatalism seen in failing to try; evidence is economic under-development	Man can and should manage and perfect nature; optimistic due to results of economic progress
National Intent	Intervention, imperialism, subversion	Sovereignty, respect, recognition	Lacking vision, discipline; needs help to reform flawed political and economic systems	Good-natured missionary, helpful, showing others "the way"
Work Ethic	Obsessive materialism, don't know how or when to relax	Work not inherently redeeming, something that must be done	Lazy, work is bad, as seen in Mexican sayings: "do not today what you can do tomorrow," and "work is sacred; don't touch it"	Work is the measure of a man, as seen in sayings "never put off until tomorrow what can be done today" and "an idle mind is the devil's workshop"

Source: *Based upon* United States and Latin America: Myths and Stereotypes of Nature and Civilization *by Frederick B. Pike, University of Texas Press, 1992.*

(text continued from page 42)

From greetings, to nonverbal expressions, to hand gestures, to the type of meetings that are preferred by executives in other cultures, the globally competent NAFTA manager is familiar with such practices making his transition appear smooth and comfortable, and instilling confidence and trust in his foreign colleagues.

"To successfully deal with a new culture, whether with a person from a specific company or a different country, you must make an effort to identify their cultural values and inherent priorities, and how they differ from your own" [14].

Table 3-2 is a brief selection of some of the differences that exist with respect to simple interpersonal protocol in Canada, Mexico, and the United States.

Culture and Interpersonal Interaction

In her insightful book, *Management in Two Cultures,* widely acknowledged cross-cultural management consultant Eva Kras has developed a framework for comparing major cultural variables as they differ between the United States and Mexico (Table 3-3).

Understanding Other Management Cultures

In the United States, Canada, and Mexico, the diversity of cultures present an enormous array of ethnicities, cuisines, attitudes, and fashions. It is more difficult to distinguish, however, how preferring a tortilla to a baguette or bun, or saying *Bonne nuit* instead of *Buenas noches* or *Good night* will affect the way members of the various NAFTA communities and cultures work together.

Given that NAFTA is first and foremost a trade agreement, regardless of what other longer term ramifications it may hold for supranational integration in North America, its most direct cultural impact will be on working men and women. The first to be affected will be the foot soldiers, those men and women who represent their companies in one of the other NAFTA countries. These individuals will need to be cognizant not only of their own cultural attitudes and biases, but also about their attitudes towards

(text continued on page 51)

Table 3-2
Intercultural Customs Survey

VARIABLE	MEXICO	USA	CANADA
Greetings	AM: *¡Buenos días!* (Good Morning) PM: *¡Buenas tardes!* (Good Afternoon) *¡Buenas noches!* (Good Night) Anytime: *¡Hola!* = Hello *¿Cómo esta?* = How are you *¡Mucho gusto!* = Nice to meet you	AM: Good morning PM: Good afternoon Good evening Good night Anytime: How are you? Fine, thanks! Hello! Hi! Nice to meet you!	English expressions generally similar to American Cheers! = Good bye French: Tu vas bien? = How are you? Bonjour = Good day
Handshake	Handshakes common, *abrazo* for close friends	Firm handshake and smile at beginning and end of formal encounter; wave of hand in informal situations	Handshake and smile at beginning and end of formal encounter; Nodding head o.k. in informal situation
Contracts	Verbal or written	Written	Written
Eye Contact	Important	Important	Less Important

table continues

47

Table 3-2 (continued)

VARIABLE	MEXICO	USA	CANADA
Business Dining	Breakfasts, and long, relaxed lunches common; deals made at end of meal; heavy food and alcohol accepted	Short lunches; business not mixed with pleasure; no alcohol	Short lunches (1–1-1/2 hours), light food, no alcohol, not to be overly enjoyed
Social Dining	Guests generally arrive one hour late	Guests arrive on time	Guests arrive on time
Punctuality	Very flexible/less punctual	Rigid/punctual	Rigid/punctual
Level of Formality	Formal	Informal	Informal
Risk Orientation	Moderate	High	Low Conservative

Speed of Decision Making	Moderate	Fast	Moderate to Slow
Language Competency	Businessmen will speak English; like dignified, respectful, eloquent language	Assume everyone speaks English; prefer practical, language; intimidated by other languages	Anglophones usually monolingual; Francophones usually bilingual; willing to try other languages
Nonverbal gestures	Close personal distance, frequent touching and hand gestures	Large distance between speakers (two ft.) Few hand gestures	Large distance between speakers, less in Quebec; Quebecois use more hand gestures

Source: *Portions based upon Culturgrams, the article "Comprenda a los Candienses" by Tim Falconer, and "Good Neighbors" by John Condon.*

49

Table 3-3
Eva Kras's Cultural Factors

FACTOR	MEXICO	U.S.
Family	Family is first priority; children sheltered; executive mobility limited	Family usually second to work; children independent; executive mobility unrestricted
Religion	Long Roman Catholic tradition; fatalistic outlook	Mixed religions; "master of own life" outlook
Pedagogical Approach	Memorization; theoretical emphasis; rigid, broad curriculum	Analytical approach; practical emphasis; narrow, in-depth specialization
Nationalism	Very nationalistic; proud of long history and traditions; reluctant to settle outside Mexico	Very patriotic; proud of "American way of life"; assumes everyone shares his/her materialistic values
Emotional Sensitivity	Sensitive to differences of opinion; fears loss of face; shuns confrontation	Separates work from emotions; sensitivity seen as weakness; puts up tough business front
Etiquette	"Old World" formality; etiquette considered the measure of breeding	Formality often sacrificed for efficiency; "let's get to the point" approach
Grooming	Dress and grooming are status symbols	As long as appearance is reasonable, performance is first
Status	Title and position more important than money in eyes of society	Money is main status indicator and is reward for achievement
Aesthetics	Aesthetic side of life is important even at work	No time for "useless frills"
Ethics	Truth tempered by need for diplomacy; truth is a relative concept	Direct yes/no answers given and expected; truth seen as absolute value

Source: *Adaptation of* Management in Two Cultures *by Eva S.Kras.*

(text continued from page 46)

work in general. The likelihood of Canadians, Mexicans, and Americans working together in the same company, inside the same corporate culture, is growing daily.

Will each national group be able to continue with its own particular cultural interpretation of the meaning of work, and with its own company-specific management style when suddenly that company or individual finds themselves in a new facility in, for example, Monterrey, Mexico, Montreal, Canada, or Montgomery, Alabama staffed almost entirely by native workers? How do the national cultures of each country affect their management styles?

Dimensions of National Culture

André Laurent, a French management researcher who analysed the behaviors and work cultural values of managers in the United States, Europe, and Asia in 1983, found that there were great variations between cultures with respect to the role of the manager. Among other things, Laurent found that managers' opinions about what organizational hierarchies were desirable, and what the nature of power within the organization should be, were strongly affected by their nationalities [15]. Indeed, Laurent found that when foreign employees worked together within the same company, the cultural differences they experienced were actually stronger than they would have been if the employees had worked at domestic companies in their own countries. Somehow, organizational culture actually magnified differences in cross-cultural work values.

Dutch researcher Geert Hofstede [16] identified four dimensions of national culture that can be used to make meaningful comparisons about the ways in which differences in national character affect management culture. The four dimensions are:

1. Power Distance — The extent to which members of a society accept that there is an unequal distribution of power in institutions and organizations.
2. Uncertainty Avoidance — The extent to which members of a society feel threatened by uncertain or ambiguous situations.

3. Individualism/Collectivism — Individualism exists when members of a society feel responsible for only themselves and their immediate family, and form only loosely knit social structures. Collectivism occurs when people distinguish between "in-groups" and "out-groups," and is characterized by strong feelings of loyalty to one's own group and the expectation that in exchange for such loyalty the group will support and protect them.

4. Masculinity — Represents the extent to which the dominant values in society stress assertiveness, money, and possessions, while not caring about others. Femininity describes cultures in which the emphasis is said to be placed upon human relationships, overall quality of life, and concern for others.

For the purposes of this discussion, a closer comparative look at the results found for Canada, Mexico, and the United States can be found in Figures 3-1 and 3-2. Figure 3-1 shows the positions of 40 countries on the power distance and uncertainty avoidance scale, and Figure 3-2 shows their positions when power distance and individualism are interfaced.

Power Distance

Mexico. In terms of power distance, Mexico ranked 38 of 40, indicating a very high tolerance for unequal distribution of power in society. This finding is augmented by the near legendary executive powers of the Mexican president, and the Mexican management style that is generally described as authoritarian and centralized.

United States. The United States ranked 15 out of 40 on power distance, indicating that while authority is accepted, employees definitely expect to participate in the sharing of power, with an atmosphere of greater trust and partnership between U.S. management and workers.

Canada. Of the 40 countries surveyed, Canada ranked 14 on power distance, indicating that, in this respect, a great similarity

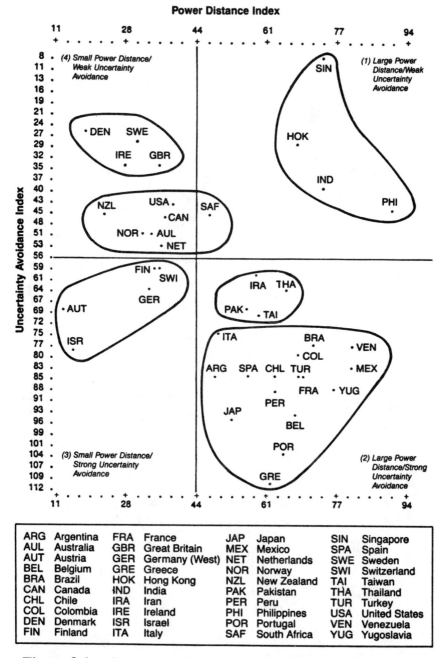

Figure 3-1. *Position of 40 countries on the power distance and uncertainty avoidance scales (From Hofstede [16]).*

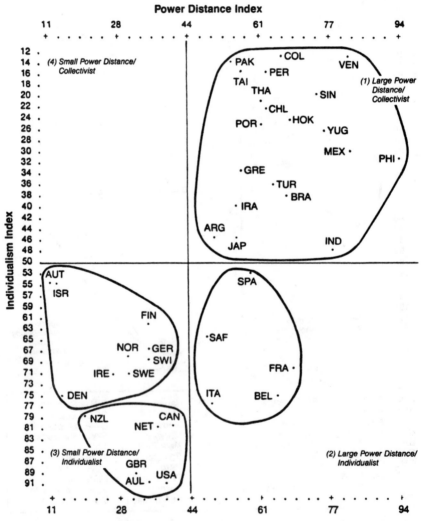

Figure 3-2. *Positions of 40 countries on the power distance and individualism scales (From Hofstede [16]).*

exists between the attitudes of U.S. and Canadian workers and managers with respect to the distribution of power.

Individualism/Collectivism

Mexico. On the scale of Individualism/Collectivism, Mexico ranked only 12 out of 40, which indicates a fairly strong leaning in favor of group versus individual loyalty. This is further reinforced by the "high context" nature of the culture, and the extraordinary importance given to preservation of relationships and face-saving in the Mexican culture.

United States. Out of the 40 countries surveyed, the United States was found to be the most individualistic. This strong sense of individualism is cultivated at a young age in American children, who are given a wide range of discretion in school regarding personal expression. Parents encourage children's independence, and by a certain age the child actually may be more influenced by their peer group than their parents. Individual achievement is seen as the measure of self worth, so Americans are willing to move to find opportunities even if that means leaving family and friends. This exists in marked contrast to the closely knit, paternalistic, extended-family structure in Mexico, upon which the realities of power distribution in many Mexican organizations are seemingly modeled.

Canada. Canada ranked 36 of 40, again attesting to the strong cultural similarities between the two Anglo-American neighbors. Canadians are shown to have significant differences with Mexicans with respect to their perceptions about organizational power sharing, as well.

"The consequences of Hofstede's conclusions are significant. Leadership, decision-making, teamwork, organization, motivation, and, in fact, everything that managers do is learned. Because management functions are learned, they are based upon assumptions about one's place in the world. Therefore, managers from other business systems are not merely "underdeveloped" managers from one's own particular country" [17].

Expanded Discussion of NAFTA Management Traits

Hofstede's four variables serve as a solid foundation for describing the core elements of cross-cultural differences, but to understand the complexity of the management challenge faced by North American managers as they enter into new interNAFTA agreements, a more detailed inspection of specific management issues directly affecting Canada, Mexico, and the United States is needed.

In his *Industrial Competitiveness and Culture in Monterrey: An Overview,* Robert B. Sinclair, a management consultant for international manufacturing operations in Mexico, developed the following framework to broaden the discussion of culture's effects on management issues between the United States and Mexico. Modified by the authors to include Canada, it represents an application of well-documented cultural values and cultural differences to the reality of today's multicultural North American workplace, and provides current insights into the nature of the differing worldviews and the cultural barriers that can be anticipated by managers of an interNAFTA workforce (Table 3-4).

NAFTA Management Insights

Equipped with the preceding paradigms for cross-national cultural comparisons, NAFTA managers will be able to foresee many of the potential cultural collisions that may be on the long road ahead to making NAFTA a success for all three member countries. Nonetheless, a concise summary of specific management issues, prepared by Eva Kras in *Management in Two Cultures* will serve to complete the picture.

Kras has identified the ten areas where national cultural differences cause the greatest impact on Mexican and American coworkers. (See Table 3-5.) These differences, related to management style and general cultural values, can have a profoundly negative impact in the workplace if they are not duly recognized and proactively addressed.

(text continued on page 65)

Table 3-4

Intercultural Management Traits

TRAIT	MEXICO	UNITED STATES	CANADA
GROUP DYNAMICS	Moderate context, ambiguous information accepted; face-saving and preservation of respect important; conformity important for maintaining a sense of community and group identity; benefit perceived for group membership via contacts	Low-context, therefore a demand for detailed information; separation of persons and task allows criticism and objectivity; community often sacrificed to promote personal gain; little perceived benefit to group membership	English is a low context language and native speakers tend to focus on clarity and preciseness; individualism is less evident in Canada than in the United States but greater than Mexico; French Canadians are more high context
PERSONAL RELATIONS	Honesty, dignity and respect viewed as measure of individual in group; a balance between "*confianza*" and ability in evaluations; information and privilege sharing limited to those who have "*confianza*" of the person providing it; personal or family relations at work considered an advantage	Individual evaluated independently of personal relationships, evaluation in workplace linked to accomplishment of tangible tasks, information and privilege offered to those who show ability; hiring of friends and family seen as unethical	The "rugged individualism" often used to describe business people from the United States does not fit the typical Canadian, whose strong values include family, traditions and pride of being Canadian

table continues

Table 3-4 (continued)

TRAIT	MEXICO	UNITED STATES	CANADA
INDIVIDU-ALISM	Upper classes may educate individual to be assertive, while lower teach patience and docility; any rebellion more likely to be in groups; personal goals pursued by balancing individual and group desires; lack of group support may limit action	Almost all are taught to be assertive, at times rebellious; personal goals based upon individual desires guided by belief in self-determinism	Canadians are somewhat between Mexicans and Americans in terms of individual aspiration versus group goals
ETHNO-CENTRISM	Manifested as pride in being part of Mexico, and/or regional community; refer to Mexicans from other regions as *"foraneos"* (foreigners), and people of other nationalities as *"extranjeros"* (strangers); concerned about national sovereignty, U.S.A. seen as threat; strong belief in nation's and region's cultural and moral superiority, yet national inferiority	Displayed as pride in being a product of the U.S.A.; belief in the superiority of racist ethnocentricity overtly the nation in virtually all fields based on the character of individuals; responded to, but still existent between various ethnic groups of multiracial society; social heterogeneity is officially embraced	The over acceptance of immigrants has made Canada a multicultural and multilinguial society; cultural diversity is apparent in most cities and is supported by legislation and programs

	is assumed in economic, technological, education, and production issues; society subtly heterogeneous based on diverse indigenous groups and racial mixes; covert belief in the inferiority of the indigenous population		Small power distance; authority can be challenged and questioned with politeness
POWER	Power a function of position, personality, and money; large power distance between leaders and subordinate; power believed to be abusive & conspiratorial by nature	Power is a function of ability to execute orders, achieve results, and money; small power distance; power is ability, and therefore should be challenged and delegated	
LEADER-SHIP	Leader responsible for all decisions, execution relegated to subordinates; criticism in leader-subordinate interchange usually taken personally, as cultural priority of maintaining relationships denies separation	A leader is a coordinator and director of the work of his/her subordinates; leaders can be questioned, but retain the final say; criticism can be personal, or impersonal, or both, depending upon the	Leadership traits are similar to the United States in many aspects; some experience feelings of inferiority when interacting with aggressive and dominant colleagues

table continues

Table 3-4 (continued)

TRAIT	MEXICO	UNITED STATES	CANADA
	of people and problems; subordinates must balance desires of various leaders, and receive little feedback; leadership granted as a result of loyalty to superiors and task-achievement; innovation is an option open only to leader; sharing power may be seen as weakness	content; leaders must balance the needs of many subordinates; leadership gained through achievement of results; leaders may delegate power to subordinates and allow innovation and not lose power	
MOTIVATION	Main motivations are money and services offered by the company; most prefer to work in a friendly atmosphere, and socialization with co-workers is high; opportunity for advancement often a secondary factor; responsibility sometimes avoided; loyalty to co-workers and firm can be high	Main motivations are money and opportunity for advancement; most prefer to work in an atmosphere of action and opportunity; socialization with co-workers is low; increased responsibility is desired; loyalty to co-workers and firm is low	High taxes and a long history of government-provided services including health care and low-cost qualtiy educaion are expected

60

EXPECTA-TIONS	Most see a limit to aspirations for advancement; expect to make a good living, cover basic needs of family, and educate children; many are content with a "stable" job; little planning for retirement, believing that continued work and family will support them in old age	Many see no end to the possibilities for advancement, and expect to continue to learn, earn, and do more throughout career; job mobility is high even in stable positions; much planning for retirement; goal is to be self-sufficient upon leaving workplace	The European influence of moderation in goals rather than unlimited lofty expectation is the norm
COMMUNITY AT WORK	Community is expected at work; top-down communication, little contact between departments due to fear of causing trouble; pyramidal organizational structure; small businesses are family-based	Community at work is downplayed, communication is top-down/bottom-up, contact between departments as needed; administration is pyramidal, small businesses not family-based	Interpersonal realtionships in and outside of work are important; administration is hierarchial
COMMUNI-CATION	Most work communication is verbal, written orders less important; face-to-face contact is key; social and work-related communication allowed	Communication is verbal and written, written highly valued; face-to-face contact not more important than memos or telephone; social talk frowned upon	Communication is verbsal and written with a behavior between high- and low-context communication styles

table continues

Table 3-4 (continued)

TRAIT	MEXICO	UNITED STATES	CANADA
LANGUAGE AS ETHNO-CENTRISM	Nearly all speak Spanish; language is important as it shows membership in the national community; dialects of minimal importance, interaction with non-speakers common; English is popular as a second language and is seen as a means to increased opportunities; adoption or adaptation of foreign words is common	Nearly all speak English; language is an identifier of citizenship; dialects of minimal importance; inter-action with non-speakers not frequent, and no second language is popular or seen as important in personal advancement; adoption of foreign words is not common	English and French are spoken by a majority of the population with at least some degree of proficiency; Italian, Chinese, Portugese, Greek, and many other languages are spoken by significant numbers

LANGUAGE IN SOCIETY	Language usages and idioms used in class identification, with differences seen along economic lines; language structure permits expression of class division in everyday speech; professional titles used in language to denote status; taboos often based on aggressive sexual references	Language usages and idioms used in class identification, differences mainly found along economic and racial lines; language permits little expression of class status; professional titles only used in the case of medical doctors; taboos based on sexual and bodily function references, as well as blasphemy	Proper language usage highly emphasized in education and contines in business; the influence of Britain is this aspect is apparent

Source: *Adaptation/Modification from "Industrial Competitiveness and Culture in Monterrey," by Robert B. Sinclair. ITESM, 1992. Modified to include Canada. Canadian variables developed by Robert T. Moran.*

63

Table 3-5
Management Styles

ASPECT	MEXICO	USA
Work/ Leisure	Works to live; leisure considered essential for full life; money is for enjoying life	Lives to work; leisure seen as reward for hard work; money often end in itself
Direction/ Delegation	Traditional managers autocratic; younger managers starting to delegate responsibility; subordinates used to being assigned tasks, not authority	Managers delegate responsibility and authority; executive seeks responsibility and accepts accountability
Theory v. Practice	Basically theoretical mind; practical implementation often difficult	Basically pragmatic mind; action-oriented problem-solving approach
Control	Still not fully accepted; sensitive to being "checked upon"	Universally accepted and practiced
Staffing	Family and friends favored because of trustworthiness; promotions based on loyalty to superiors	Relatives usually barred; favoritism is not acceptable; promotion based upon performance
Loyalty	Mostly loyal to superior (person rather than organization); beginnings of self-loyalty	Mainly self-loyalty; performance motivated by ambition
Competition	Avoids personal competition; favors harmony at work	Enjoys proving her/ himself in competitive situations
Training and Development	Training highly theoretical; few structured programs	Training concrete, specific; structured programs general
Time	Relative concept; deadlines flexible	Categorical imperative; deadlines and commitments are firm

Table 3-5 (continued)

ASPECT	MEXICO	USA
Planning	Mostly short-term because of uncertain environment	Mostly long-term in stable environment

Source: *Adaptation of* Management in Two Cultures, *by Eva S.Kras.*

(text continued from page 56)

Summary

Three distinctly different nations, each with its own national character and cultural values, comprise what is now known as the North American Free Trade zone. Culture is a tool that individuals in each of these societies use to make daily decisions and make sense of the world that confronts them.

Cultural identity and perceived superiority also can be used to justify prejudice, stereotypes, and racism, all of which penalize the positive and productive interaction of the societies engaged in their use. Through a familiarization with, and understanding of, historical stereotypes from both sides, these roadblocks can be removed so that today's globally minded NAFTA manager can forge profitable human relationships based on direct experience and objective facts obtained from personal encounters, as opposed to cynical historical hearsay.

Armed with insights into the day-to-day business protocol in each of the three countries, managers will have the necessary interpersonal insights that will assist them in making the ever-so-important positive first impression.

Hofstede's four variables provide the manager with a new vocabulary for objectively and incisively discussing cross-cultural differences between many countries, and Sinclair's framework focuses these newly acquired tools directly back on the issue of culture in Canada, Mexico, and the United States.

Finally, Eva Kras's management style comparison chart brings the global manager into the office, where he or she gains direct insight into the very issues that can be so costly should they be allowed to come between NAFTA's managers.

NAFTA's future, and all the benefits that it will bring to the citizens of the three great member countries, depends on the resolve of each and every company and manager to make human relationships work. You can plug in a machine, but you can't just plug in a person.

References

1. Garreau, J. *The Nine Nations of North America.* New York: Avon Books, 1982, p. xvi.
2. Moran, R.T. and Stripp, W.G. *Dynamics of Successful International Business Negotiations.* Houston: Gulf Publishing Co., 1991, p. 43.
3. Ferraro, Gary. *The Cultural Dimension of International Business.* New York: Prentice Hall, 1990, page 18.
4. Harris, P.R. and Moran, R.T. *Managing Cultural Differences.* Houston: Gulf Publishing Co., 1991, p. 212.
5. Ibid.
6. Ibid., p. 212.
7. Ibid.
8. Ibid.
9. Campbell, J. *The Power of Myth.* New York: Doubleday, 1988, p. 4.
10. Moran, R.T. and Stripp, W.G. *Dynamics of Successful International Business Negotiations.* Houston: Gulf Publishing Co., 1991, p. 53.
11. Pike, F.B. *The United States and Latin America: Myths and Stereotypes of Civilization and Nature.* Austin: University of Texas Press, 1992.
12. Ibid. p. 46.
13. Campbell, J. *The Power of Myth.* New York: Doubleday, 1988, p. 13.
14. Elashmawi, F. and Harris, P.R. *Multicultural Management.* Houston: Gulf Publishing Co., 1993, p. 46.
15. Laurent. A., "The Cultural Diversity of Western Conceptions of Management." *International Studies of Management and Organization,* Vol. XIII, No. 1-2, Spring-Summer 1983, p. 77.

16. Hofstede, G. *Culture's Consequences: International Differences in Work Related Values.* Beverly Hills: Sage Publishing, 1984.
17. Harris, P.R. and Moran, R.T. *Managing Cultural Differences.* Houston: Gulf Publishing Co., 1991, p. 88.

Situations Illustrating Cross-Cultural Interactions

This chapter is divided into two sections. The first part contains a number of "Commentaries." These are short excerpts from the printed media in Canada, the United States, and Mexico and represent certain viewpoints and perspectives on the relationship between Canadians, Americans, and Mexicans in the context of NAFTA.

The second part of the chapter presents short case studies or situations illustrating interactions between persons of the three countries. The understandings to be drawn from each situation are clear.

Commentaries

Mexicans earn less than Americans and Canadians. But their manufacturers are less efficient, their interest rates are higher, and their freight charges steeper. Lower wages alone will not make Mexican companies competitive. Success will depend on productivity gains, intelligent investment, and agile management—the same factors, in short, that will determine the success of firms north of the Rio Grande. If they do not succeed, Ross Perot's 'giant sucking sound' will be that of even more illegal immigrants going north.

The Economist
October 9, 1993

'Far from exporting American jobs, manufacturing overseas for overseas markets creates American jobs,' management expert Peter F.

Drucker has noted. Exporting and manufacturing abroad complement each other. For example, three-fourths of the value of Ford Motor Company's Mercury Tracers and Ford Escorts assembled at its Hermosillo plant come from the United States. Victor M. Barreiro, president and general director of Ford's Mexican operations, has stated that 'we are, in fact, creating jobs in the U.S.'

> David A. Heenan, "After
> NAFTA: The Long-Term
> Benefits," *Journal of*
> *Business Strategy*
> March/April 1993

A 1994 Conference Board Study of over 500 CEOs from Canada, Mexico, and the United States found:

Well over two-thirds of the CEOs in all three participating countries believe that NAFTA will improve business conditions in their respective nations. U.S., and particularly Mexican executives, are somewhat more optimistic than their counterparts in Canada.

> "The Conference Board:
> Chief Executives Assess
> NAFTA, CEO Opinions
> from Canada, Mexico
> and the U.S."
> January 1994, Number 10

Douglas Clark says that when he emerged from a recent 45-minute business meeting in Mexico City, his Mexican driver was worried. The driver, Clark recalls, was convinced that something had gone terribly wrong because the meeting was so short. Said Clark, president of the Northern Telecom subsidiary based in Mexico City, 'I had to reassure him that everything was fine—that it is possible to do business in that time.'

The Mexican emphasis on strong personal relations in business, which tends to lead to long meetings and even longer lunches, is just one of the differences encountered by Canadians exploring those markets in anticipation of the North American Free Trade Agreement (NAFTA).

> *MacLean's*
> December 14, 1992

One Canadian company that learned about the potential for cultural clashes the hard way is Bombardier Ltd. of Montreal. After buying a railcar from the Mexican government in April, Bombardier was outraged when its bid for a $150-million contract to build subway cars for Mexico City's transit authority failed in August. Said one senior Canadian government official who helped to smooth ensuing furor, 'Bombardier had no grasp of the local business culture and no established presence in the market—so they grossly miscalculated.'

> *MacLean's*
> December 14, 1992

Americans look to NAFTA for its potential effects on jobs and economic well-being, but for Mexicans it is a tangle of emotional issues. Jobs and economic stimuli are important to them, but so are the underlying questions of trust, fairness, equality, and neighborliness.

> Tod Robberson, "NAFTA
> Seen as Equalizer," *The*
> *Washington Post*
> November 12, 1992

America has never had a neighbor of the importance Mexico will acquire in the next century—with or without NAFTA. By then it will be a country with a population of more than 100 million and equal to the Asian 'little tigers,' such as Korea. Our de facto open borders make friendly relations a vital national interest. Twenty-million Mexican residents in the United States link the interest of the two nations on the human level. The healthier Mexico's economy, the lower the illegal immigration and the greater U.S. exports will be to an economy whose propensity to import from us is the highest in the world.

> Henry A. Kissinger, "With
> NAFTA, U.S. Finally
> Creates a New World
> Order," *Los Angeles Times*
> July 18, 1993

. . . (a) familiar complaint by foreigners doing business in Mexico: Even under reform-minded President Carlos Salinas de Gortari, bribes are a standard operating procedure and there is no legal recourse for those who buck the system.

> David Clark Scott,
> "Mexican Corruption and
> NAFTA," *The Christian
> Science Monitor*
> April 8, 1993

. . . As the two economies converge, can Mexico eradicate the bribery that has long been a fact of its business life? And how will newly arrived U.S. companies, banned by law from making foreign payoffs, cope with Mexico's different legal and ethical climate?

> Peter Behr, "Corruptions
> Issue Enters the NAFTA
> Debate," *The Washington
> Post*, October 27, 1993

Just as in the United States and Canada, Mexico will have its winners and losers. Amazingly, in this case it seems as if those who have been deprived for so long will now gain the most, while those who have traditionally preyed on Mexican society will finally get their comeuppance. John Wayne would like that.

> Richard Seid, "Mexicans
> and NAFTA," *The
> Christian Science Monitor*
> January 6, 1993

. . . Mexicans accept the fact that free trade will be good for the economy, but they have visceral worries about how it will affect things like sovereignty, culture, and morality, says Federico San Roman, a psychiatrist and newspaper columnist.

> Matt Moffett, "With Gloria
> Trevi in Mexico, Madonna
> Might Fear NAFTA," *The
> Wall Street Journal*
> November 16, 1993

Gilbert Cisneros, president of the Rocky Mountain Chapter of the U.S.-Mexico Chamber of Commerce states:

It takes time to build relationships in Mexico. . . . They have to have confidence that you will be around. Make contacts with associations in the Mexican marketplace.

> Brian Baron and Rick
> Mendosa, "Healing the
> Wounds of NAFTA,"
> *Hispanic Business*
> January 1994

Stephen Clarkson, a political scientist at the University of Toronto states:

The American civilization is a powerful one, but it is the most primitive, violent and unappealing of the great civilizations of the world. . . . Canada has always been a kinder, gentler society, with stronger European roots and a much more diverse population. . . . The future is not nearly so bright for the Mexican managerial class. With notable exceptions, they simply lack the tools, the temperament, or the will to be competitive with managers of the first-world firms. The former protectionist system allowed them liberties of mediocrity which will not be available in the near future.

> Richard Seid, "Mexicans
> and NAFTA," *The*
> *Christian Science Monitor*
> January 6, 1994

As Octavio Paz once observed, the Mexicans are people who inhabit their bodies, whereas the rest of North American does not. The mental climate of the country is still permeated by the feeling and outlook of the indigenous population, which is close to the rhythms of nature . . .

> Morris Berman, "Shadow
> across the Rio Grande,"
> *Resurgence*
> March/April 1990

The Case Study Method of Learning

Case studies are widely used in educational settings. Harvard Business School uses case studies in many courses, as do many executive training programs. This method of learning and problem solving from real business situations has been demonstrated as effective.

The cases that follow are short mini-cases, each describing a real issue. Some of the situations are based on conflicts and others are based on an approach to business relationships. We recommend that the reader draw from each mini-case the appropriate learning and application. All mini-cases are based on actual and recent situations.

Mini-Case One: Securing a Job in a Mexican Bank[1]

With six months until graduation and summer break in front of me, I arrived in Mexico with a briefcase full of resumes and an extensive list of references from previous employers. I felt that a strategy of showing commitment to Mexico by living there would help me earn their *confianza,* or trust. I quickly realized that I had underestimated the importance of relationships in Mexico.

Getting interviews was easy. I also learned that my experience was valuable; but what I did not anticipate was that my references, for all intents and purposes, were useless . . . they were from strangers.

At first, employment application in Mexico appears to be cumbersome. Questions such as ages and occupations of siblings may seem trivial to an American, but to a Mexican it demonstrates a candidate's family background and connections. I learned that nepotism in Mexico is expected rather than criticized.

After several meetings with seemingly apathetic recruiters, I changed my strategy. I asked Mexican friends if I could use them as references, and chose family friends, who knew little of my professional qualities, to attest to my character and education. None of my "references" worked in the industry that I did, but I was told that this wasn't critical. I finally felt that I was being taken seriously.

---

[1] This mini-case was written by Roland Clough, a graduate of the American Graduate School of International Management.

This feeling was short-lived. While I did progress farther along in the interview process, I rarely made it past the personnel department. To me this was symptomatic of the latin people's discomfort in saying "no" directly to someone. In other words, they went through the motions because I had some connections, but these connections fell short of what I needed to get to the next level.

During my last week in Mexico, in the summer of 1993, I was able to speak with the director of a division that was hiring new people. We met for a half hour, during which time I explained in detail why I wanted to live and work in Mexico. Apparently he was satisfied, so we discussed my qualifications as they would serve the company. He wanted me to meet with another group, but there was not enough time, so we agreed to keep in touch.

By now I had learned my lesson in terms of the value of relationships in Mexico. I decided to try to build a relationship with the person whom, I hoped, would eventually be able to help me. I called him frequently, sent him several articles related to his business, but most importantly, I recalled that he wanted to study English in the United States, and I located a school where he could. I also knew an important executive who had studied in the same program, and I asked him to inform my Mexican potential employer of the program. This was yet another way of showing him that I was connected and therefore good for his firm.

I thought I was "in." I had covered experience, relations, and connections, but I still could not get him to commit to me. His secretary told me that he recently had surgery, and I used this as a vehicle to show my concern for his health (legitimately so), while stroking his ego. This worked because he finally invited me for a meeting to discuss salary.

I did my homework on the market and ascertained my value in Mexico prior to meeting with him. This is not always easy, but it is possible, at least, to arrive at a salary range.

Staying with my relation-based strategy, I again dedicated most of my energy to building the relationship. When I was introduced to other directors, I attempted to sell "us" rather than "me." I am certain that when it finally came time to negotiate salary, their input was considered and I was accommodated—already considered an "insider."

I do not propose that this strategy will work in any or every job search overseas. What I am certain of, however, is that a thorough study of the culture is critical, and that one must be flexible enough to accept the idiosyncracies of that culture and to play by their rules. In any culture, we usually base our sales pitch on our perception of what is important to employers. The only perception that counts, however, is theirs.

Mini-Case Two: Getting to Know You[2]

John Trygstad looked at his watch for the third time in an hour. He had a plane to catch out of Leon and needed to get an answer to close the deal to buy a small, local, textile plant. He had made this trip after initial telephone and fax contact, as well as some third-party mediation. John was told you needed to take time in Mexico to build relationships, so he scheduled four days in Leon, to show his interest, and to let Carlos Suarez Mier, the plant owner, get to know him. Even after four days, he still hadn't gotten a straight answer from Carlos about a commitment to sell the plant.

On his first day in town he was taken out for a fantastic dinner. The second day he met Carlos at the plant for what he thought would be negotiations, but instead he was given a tour of the plant and then of the town. On day three Carlos took him to see a soccer game won by the company team. Carlos reminded him of the win on more than one occasion. At the game, and the dinner following, John met some of the civic leaders and local suppliers, all of whom seemed to respect Carlos. Today they were back at the plant, but Carlos had insisted on a second plant tour during the middle of discussions about the deal. John appreciated Carlos' pointing out the recent capital improvements and the

---

[2] This mini-case was written by Dr. David Braaten, Associate Professor of International Studies at the American Graduate School of International Management, Glendale, Arizona.

neatness of the personnel, but he had a deal to finalize and didn't feel like giving any more compliments.

Besides all this, trying to negotiate with Carlos was frustrating. He never followed one point of discussion to the end. He constantly changed topics, talking about the soccer team, the relations he had with the suppliers and how efficient they were, the town, his family members who worked in management at the plant, and other mundane subjects, as well as asking several personal questions. Why couldn't he just stick to discussing the deal John was tying to get down on paper? With time passing, John was either going to have to take the deal as now presented or let it slip away. In all of this, he still wasn't sure what Carlos was going to do. But John did know one thing: either way, this was the last time he was going to invest so much time, effort, and money in a deal in Mexico.

Mini-Case Three: An American in Canada[3]

Having worked with numerous clients in Ontario, Susan felt she was familiar with Canadian business practices and culture. As a representative with a New York-based subcontractor, Susan had had the opportunity to work with a variety of Canadian builders and developers. During her assignments she had learned about Canadian culture and how it affected her business relationships. She had learned, for instance, that patience paid off, as Canadian business people made decisions at a slower pace than she was used to in New York. She also knew that Canadians placed great importance on family life, and as such, did not spend as many weekends working at the office as she did. Finally, she had observed that Canadians were somewhat more conservative in outlook than were her American business partners.

When a new project in Quebec came her way, she felt comfortable in taking it. While she was aware of the language related differences between the Quebecoise and the non-French speaking

---

[3] This mini-case was written by Tammy Waidelich, a graduate student at the American Graduate School of International Management.

majority of Canada, she did not expect such a profound difference in culture.

While setting up meetings with clients was not a problem, actually having a meeting on time was. Susan soon learned that even though her clients took these meetings seriously, they did not consider punctuality of utmost importance, often arriving fifteen minutes to half an hour late. She also found French Canadians to be even more reserved upon initial encounter than their English-speaking counterparts. Once she had established a relationship, however, she felt that the French Canadians warmed up quickly.

Mini-Case Four: Cultural Influences[4]

John Cates had heard the joke about Canadian-American relations before. Referring to the close relationship that existed between former Canadian Prime Minister Brian Mulroney and former U.S. President George Bush, it was often said of Mulroney that he would say "yes" to George Bush before the telephone even rang.

For many Canadians, this was no laughing matter. In a country whose population was one-tenth that of their powerful neighbor to the south, this "joke" summed up the concerns many Canadians had regarding their relationship with the United States. At one end of the spectrum, many Canadians felt they were being taken for granted by their American ally. At the other end, many felt that Canada often was regarded as a lesser copy of the United States.

Having grown up in Windsor, Ontario, a border city just south of Detroit, Michigan, John saw things differently. He felt fortunate to have lived in "the best of both worlds." John was proud of his Canadian heritage. He had studied business law at University with an eye on America. At the same time, living near the border enabled him to get to know American culture and values firsthand. John put this knowledge to good use. In the same year that he graduated, the Canada-U.S. Free Trade Agreement was

---

[4] This mini-case was written by Tammy Waidelich, a graduate student at the American Graduate School of International Management.

signed. Together with two friends with whom he had graduated, John formed a consulting firm to advise Canadian and American business people on inter-American trade.

With several years of experience under his belt, John feels he is well positioned to help clients meet the challenges and opportunities of the recently signed North American Free Trade Agreement. John feels he owes much of his success to "growing up with both cultural influences in my life."

Mini-Case Five: Work Force Productivity[5]

Four years ago, Quality Coils, a producer of electromagnetic coils, closed its factory in Bristol, Connecticut and opened a new one in Juarez, Mexico. The motivation for this move was Mexico's low wage rates, which were roughly one-third what Americans were paid by the firm.

But high absenteeism, low productivity, and problems with long distance management resulted in regular losses for the firm. It was true that the factory could hire three Mexican employees for the cost of one American, but to accomplish the work that one person in Connecticut had done, three Mexicans were needed. The company had overlooked the many other factors that affected business operations and could reduce the savings achieved by lower wage rates. These included congested roads, outdated machinery, ineffective management, poor education, and corrupt judges. Quality Coils had neglected to consider other factors, such as the skills of the work force, the quality of transportation, and the access to technology.

From the beginning, the Mexican plant encountered problems. The customers expected to continue the buying practices they had established with Quality Coils' U.S. factory. To maintain low inventories, they preferred ordering small quantities (of several thousand coils each) and expected delivery within 30 days. But the Mexican operations were not accustomed to such flexible manufacturing requirements. The materials supply problems that

---

[5] This mini-case was written by Sylvia Krieg, a graduate student at the American Graduate School of International Management.

resulted became unmanageable because they could produce only long runs of the simplest products. To further complicate the operations, shipments of components would be held at the border for weeks, delaying production.

The Mexican workers realized that the parent company was dissatisfied with their productivity. Consequently, whenever American managers visited the site (usually attempting to measure worker output), they temporarily increased their output. The Americans made numerous attempts to encourage the workers to raise productivity. They offered the workers who exceeded their production quotas coupons that could be used to buy food in local supermarkets. They tried ultimatums, requiring each employee to run 2,000 coils a week (equal to their American counterparts), but the Mexicans rarely managed more than 1,000, taking far longer to set up the machine and maintain it so it was operating fewer hours each day.

Because many of the workers had come from small villages, Quality Coils also had problems in retaining its work force. After a Christmas holiday nearly half of the plant's 50 employees did not return. They were homesick and remained in their towns in the interior of Mexico. Because this happened often, the company was continually training new employees, and this negated any productivity gains.

Finally, after four long years of frustration, Quality Coils closed the Mexican operation. Production resumed at the Connecticut factory and many of the American workers who had been laid off were rehired.

Mini-Case Six: Distribution and Sales in Mexico[6]

The largest floor products distributor in the American Southwest, Long Distribution, saw the potential for quick profits by expanding sales into the Mexican market. They simply tried to extend their American distribution system and philosophy to include northern Mexico.

---

[6] This case was written by Jeffrey D. Abbott with assistance and information supplied by Joseph A. Hostler who serves the maquiladora industry in El Paso, Texas-Ciudad Juarez, Chihuahua metropolitan area.

The company targeted Hermosillo as the first market to be opened, where Jaime, the established market leader, controlled the local market. In exchange for the contacts and penetration that he could offer, he wanted exclusive rights to the products Long distributed.

All of the smaller retailers wanted exclusivity as well. Because many businesses in Mexico are privately owned and operated, it was hard at first to know which were truly important in the market.

Despite the obvious advantages of having a local partner, Long wanted to be an American-style distributor in Mexico, insisting upon maintaining exclusive distribution rights to there products and selling to Mexican retailers from their Phoenix-based warehouse. They did not want to grant exclusivity to anyone, even if this meant sacrificing the opportunity to ally themselves with the best potential partner in the market.

Joe Hostler was a border sales specialist for Long. Long spent at least $2,000 every time they sent Joe to Mexico. Consequently, they wanted some immediate returns on this investment. Hostler knew it was extremely important for Long to find a local partner to help their sales. If a local partner could not be found, it would be necessary to make a substantial investment in warehousing facilities in Hermosillo.

Long was also reluctant to trust a Mexican partner, and would not grant exclusivity to anyone. When they encountered problems, instead of looking for a Mexican solution, they looked for an American solution, which was not effective because they had not made the effort to understand Mexican culture, business practices, or consumer preferences. Frustration mounted at Long.

During this period of indecision and lack of vision, Jaime, the market leader in Hermosillo, made a bold move. He went directly to the international division of the same carpet mill that long represented in the U.S. and obtained distribution rights to the same carpets that Long offered, effectively cutting them out of the market. Long was left with only a fraction of the customers that it spent thousands of dollar to develop.

American and Canadian companies seeking to sell or distribute in Mexico should adapt their current systems and methods to the

Mexican market. To be successful, more is needed than better prices and a bilingual salespeople. Qualified support staff within the company and guidance from a local partner in Mexico is critical. Most importantly, a commitment must be made to respect and understand the uniqueness of the Mexican market.

Mini-Case Seven: Us Against Them[7]

As Marc-Andre Rollet boarded the plane, he contemplated the negotiations he had just completed.

It had not been easy to schedule the meetings, since he had been unknown to his Mexican contacts, but seeing how successful other Quebec firms had been in the southern country encouraged him to try. One reason it was so difficult was because Mexicans typically did not return phone calls, unless the caller had been introduced first.

For both Canada and Mexico, the United States represents an aggressor; initially it was in terms of territory and today it is in terms of economy. This has resulted in a camaraderie between these nations, an "us against them" sentiment. Two common complaints are that the Americans have a superiority complex and act as if what is good for them is good for everyone else, and that they take their northern and southern neighbors for granted.

This feeling is even more intense for the French-speaking Canadians from Quebec. They feel closer to the Mexicans than they do to their countrymen, because of the animosity over Quebec's independence movement. Moreover, these Canadians are accustomed to doing business in a second language, making it easier for each party to feel sympathetic to the cultural differences.

Marc-Andre reminisced about the long process he had just concluded. Beginning with working hard to open doors, he had invested much time and energy into getting to know his Mexican counterparts. He learned the importance of getting to know and trust each other and of showing an interest in the other's family, which is considered very important to the Mexican.

---

[7] This case was written by Sylvia Krieg, a graduate student at the American Graduate School of International Management.

One of his most important lessons had been that "no" doesn't always mean no, and "yes" doesn't necessarily mean yes, either. He had expected the Mexican government automatically to grant him a contract when he purchased a manufacturing facility, simply assuming that the government would continue to purchase the same products from the factory that it had for years. However, the government expected him to pursue their business actively. As a result, the government found a new supplier.

Mini-Case Eight: Facilitating Negotiations[8]

The North American Steel Council (NASC) was composed of representatives from the iron and steel industries in the United States, Canada, and Mexico. The NASC was to identify areas of common interest and possible difficulties in the iron and steel industry in the upcoming NAFTA. Because Canadian and American representatives of the iron and steel industries had been involved with the Foreign Trade Agreement (FTA), they were acquainted and familiar with each other.

As president of the Foreign Trade Committee of the Mexican Iron and Steel Industry Association, I knew it was fundamental to meet my counterparts for many reasons, but most importantly because marked differences existed between the Mexican iron and steel industry and the U.S. and Canadian industries.

During visits with my counterparts, I became aware that, although Mexico had not participated extensively in negotiations of this type, I did have sufficient knowledge of concepts, tools, and institutions to take part effectively in discussions, and to report to my counterparts the structure and performance of the Mexican iron and steel industry.

Furthermore, the informal discussions with Americans and Canadians who I visited, who were intermediaries for their

---

[8] The information for this mini-case was provided by Dr. Rafael R. Rubio, Ph.D., who currently serves as subdirector of the Economic Studies and International Marketing Department of HYLSA Corporation, the Steel Division of the ALFA Industrial Group, one of Mexico's most important conglomerates. Translated by Jeffrey Abbott.

respective industries, opened an alternative channel of communication that enabled me to filter opinions or difficulties during the negotiation process. This eliminated unnecessary friction and delays during the actual negotiations.

Return visits to Mexico by American representatives of the industry allowed me to strengthen my interpersonal relationships by accompanying them on tours of Mexican facilities.

The work of the NASC proved to be successful for all three industries. The NASC is now a forum for consultation and discussion of issues affecting the industry. Because the group has continued to function, our relationships have been reinforced, our friendships have developed, and we are facilitating work generated by the NAFTA.

Summary

A reflection and analysis of the above mini-cases will assist persons in managing cultural differences between Canadians, Americans, and Mexicans. The cases are in no way exhaustive but can serve as a basis for the development of effective cross-cultural interactions.

Strategies for Success

Americans look to NAFTA for its potential effects on jobs and economic well-being, but for Mexicans it is a tangle of emotional issues. Jobs and economic stimuli are important to them, but so are the underlying questions of trust, fairness, equality and neighborliness.

> Tod Robberson, "NAFTA
> Seen as Equalizer," *The*
> *Washington Post*
> November 12, 1992

Workers in the global village are beginning to recognize that unless they unite with one another, they will all become losers.

> William Greider, "A
> 2,000-mile Love Canal,"
> *Rolling Stone*
> September 3, 1992

It seems to me that the personal traits of Mexican workers and management will have a great deal to do with the degree of success each sector will have in coping with the coming openness of this continent's economies.

> Richard Seid, "Mexicans
> and NAFTA," *The*
> *Christian Science Monitor*
> January 6, 1993

The case studies in Chapter Five are considerably longer than he mini-cases in the previous chapter. Each case includes an analysis and a conclusion. In each, there are a number of important considerations for those in NAFTA who wish to understand their partners.

Case One: International Technology and Human Resource Transfer[1]

Introduction

As NAFTA becomes more fully implemented, increasingly more Canadian and American executives will relocate to Mexico. Most often, managers are relocated due to their technical expertise, which is needed to organize the startup of a new plant, or to effect the transfer of technology crucial to the business' success.

"Ironically," states Rhona Statland de Lopez in an article entitled "Moving to Mexico," which appeared in the May, 1992, edition of *Business Mexico,* "with all the effort and expense involved in the selection, training, and transfer of employees to Mexico, few companies realize the importance of preparing the employee and family for the move. As a result, some business people return home prematurely because of personal or family inability to adjust to life in another country" [1].

Case Analysis

When Tom's employer, a large Canadian telecommunications firm, announced that the Toronto based factory which he had managed for the past two years would be relocated to Monterrey, Mexico, it offered the opportunity to manage the technology transfer and the start-up of the new operations. The firm offered an attractive relocation package which, in addition to his actual salary, included a healthy living allowance that would cover

---

[1] This case was supplied by Robert B. Sinclair, a management consultant for international manufacturing operations in Mexico. Mr. Sinclair has previously worked in the coordination of the implementation and certification of quality assurance systems in the maquiladora industry, and is a former Fulbright-Garcia Robles grantee to that country. The introduction and conclusion were written by Jeffrey D. Abbott.

almost all expenses, and the use of a company car. Upon completing the two-year contract, Tom figured, his stock in the company would be high. As an ex-"overseas" manager, he would be eligible for promotion to divisional production manager.

Upon arriving in Monterrey, Tom was pleased to find that the transferred operations would be supported by world-class industrial facilities, a seemingly enthusiastic work force, and a large supply of technically competent, English-speaking engineers. Corporate human resources helped ease the transfer by sending Tom and his wife to one day of cultural training and enrolling them in Spanish classes.

When small-scale production started in May, Tom's problems were mainly related to communication with his technical staff (none of whom had any cultural training). Nevertheless, the project was on schedule: all the technology had been transferred successfully and he had developed a core staff of three manufacturing supervisors with good English skills who were knowledgeable about the technical side of production.

Soon, however, a new facet was added to Tom's work: human resource management of production personnel. When Tom started production, 60 line workers were hired, none of whom spoke English. Tom's own Spanish skills had stagnated, as the pressure of keeping the project moving had obliged him to drop Spanish classes. His learning had been slow, anyway, and support for his cultural and language training from the Corporate Human Resources Department had evaporated after the first week.

Rather than attempt to communicate with 60 employees in a language with which he was not proficient, Tom delegated significant authority to his supervisors, allowing their leadership among the employees to free-up his time to administrate the operations. He was shocked to find, however, that his supervisors avoided the responsibility of innovation, and continued to look to him for all important decisions. They were reluctant even to give opinions about how to solve manufacturing problems.

When the quality department attempted to implement a quality assurance program, Tom delegated the responsibility to his supervisors. Without his presence to ratify necessary major decisions, many important activities were left undefined. The quality assurance program was abandoned. The personal reinforcement that had worked so well in Canada to motivate workers seemed to have no effect on his Mexican engineers, who were fluent in English. Perhaps a co-worker's ability to speak English did not mean that he/she thought as you did.

In October, the work force topped the 200 line-worker mark. Suddenly, the plant was larger than Tom could handle, given that he still could not manage to communicate effectively with the workers or ensure that the production supervisors would show the initiative necessary to address the many problems that erupted. The plant suffered from quality problems, witnessed by a series of customer complaints and defective products that forced the suspension of production activities for more than a week.

As an experienced manufacturing manager, Tom realized that many of the quality-related problems could be traced back to the lack of Spanish-language manufacturing and quality control documentation: resources that it had been the goal of the aborted quality assurance program to create. The vast size of the project, and the fact that the needed documentation and visual aids would have to have been in Spanish, meant that despite him being the only one technically capable of initiating the project, Tom simply could not lead the project with the level of detail necessary.

Tom remained convinced that his production supervisors had the potential to make the quality assurance project a success, but his incomplete understanding of the Mexican work culture prevented him from winning their much needed cooperation. Tom became increasingly confused and depressed, unaware of the source of his problems, while conditions at the plant continued to deteriorate. Finally, in December, with one year left in his contract, Tom resigned, leaving behind months of confusion and a manufacturing operation with serious problems.

Conclusion

"No matter how well conceived financially, an operation will not achieve its full potential, or indeed in many cases may not succeed at all, unless the human aspect is given its full due" [2]. Perhaps the most important investment a company can make in ensuring a relocated manager's success is to provide him/her with adequate pre-departure language and cultural training, and to continue to support this training after relocation is completed. Despite this fact, according to Patricia Grattan, a Mexico City-based International Relocation Consultant, "Ninety-five percent of companies don't give their workers any orientation at all. The need for orientation becomes apparent when families who view their move to Mexico as a step up the corporate ladder begin to flounder for lack of counseling about what they may expect in their new environment" [3].

Case Two: Employee Empowerment: A Canadian Success in Mexico[2]

The adaptation of management systems across cultures can be at once a challenging and frustrating process, especially so when the very concepts around which the system is structured assume the presence of, or are dependent upon, certain cultural and work values that may or may not be present in the country of application.

A situation that illustrates this well is trying to bring participative management to Mexico, because, for many reasons, Mexican workers often do not readily accept empowerment unless it is adapted to their culture in a way that they can accept and with which they can feel comfortable.

At a Canadian automotive parts supplier for the North American auto industry, an empowerment program was developed that has achieved very satisfactory results and earned the company an endorsement as a high-quality supplier eligible for direct shipment to its major customer, without intervention by the home plant.

According to the Director General, the labor-intensiveness of the company's production made it imperative to instill in the workers the confidence that each one of them was capable of being a quality inspector who had the right to refuse to accept inferior workmanship from a previous stage in the production.

---

[2] This case was written by Jeffrey D. Abbott, with information provided by a Canadian auto parts manufacturer located in Saltillo, Coahuila, Mexico.

A noted characteristic of Mexican culture, however, was the desire to preserve warm relations with colleagues, which engendered a strong unwillingness to confront another worker with his mistakes. A comment intended to be constructive and objective might likely be taken personally, and the confronted worker would feel that he had been offended. Therefore, the company needed to develop a way to take the need for personal conflict out of quality improvement.

Originated in Japan, the rotating team production concept has gained popularity in Canada and the United States as an effective method of developing quality through quality awareness. Each worker periodically rotates with his team through all of the production stages, thereby becoming intimately familiar with every aspect of the process. As a result, he is better able to recognize errors in workmanship as well as their likely cause and point of origination within the process. By requiring workers to perform various different tasks, boredom is reduced and job interest is heightened. An additional and crucial benefit has accrued to this system in Mexico at the plant, in that by organizing workers into teams, the cultural unwillingness to confront others about errors in their work has been depersonalized.

The workers spend week-long rotations in the following five production stages:

STAGE 1: Preparation of Raw Materials for processing (20 percent of work force)
STAGE 2: Raw Materials are processed into components for assembly (20 percent of work force)
STAGE 3: Assembly (20 percent of work force) Note: Steps 3 and 4 are identical
STAGE 4: Assembly (20 percent of workforce)
STAGE 5: Trim materials are added, products are packed for shipment (20 percent of workforce)

Figure 5-1 represents the five stages in the production process.

To increase quality and develop team identity, each team must select a name for itself. Teams also participate in ongoing five week competitions that test them in the following categories:

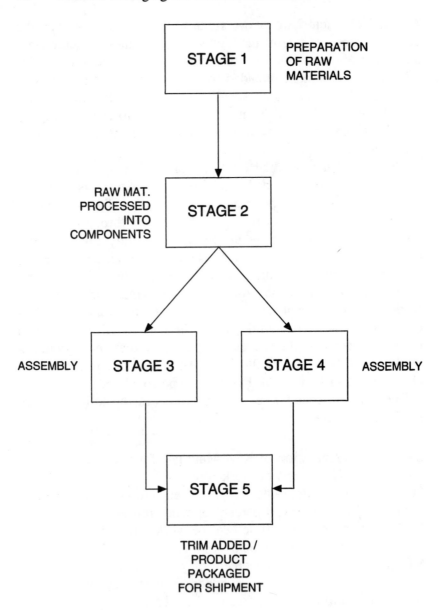

NOTE: ONE TEAM PER STAGE, 15 WORKERS PER TEAM

Figure 5-1. *Five Stages in the Production Process.*

Quality:	as measured by number of identified defects per group, per area
Production:	volume
Cleanliness:	of work area
Scrap:	waste of raw materials in preparation for processing
Efficiency:	the planning of material usage to increase above standard the supply of raw materials to production.

In each of the above five areas, all employees of the team that scores the highest get a 2 percent tax-free (bonos) salary bonus throughout the ensuing five week period. It is conceivable, but unlikely, that one team could win all five categories.

The Director General identified three steps that were essential in the implementation of work teams at this company, each of which relates to one of the three levels of workers involved: Team Supervisors, Team Leaders, and Workers.

Step One: Working with Team Supervisors to convince them to delegate their authority to the Team Leaders, and to encourage them to work *with* the Team Leaders. Mexico has been characterized as a society with an extremely high "power distance," the measure of a culture's acceptance of unequal distribution of power in society. The traditionally authoritarian Mexican manager often has guarded jealously his own skill set, and the information to which he has access, instead of using the same to develop the employees for which he is responsible. The message that supervisors are expected to delegate authority had to come straight from the Director General.

Step Two: Reassuring Team Leaders that they have the necessary skills to make decisions at their level, as well as the direct mandate of the Director General that they do so. They are told to expect that their supervisor will delegate to them the necessary latitude to allow them to make decisions. As in all management transformations, employees must be made to know that it is the express and ardent desire of the Director that the prescribed changes take place.

Step Three: Convincing the Workers that they have the authority to say "no," that they do not have to unquestionably accept everything that they are told, and that it is desirable that they ask questions and make suggestions. Most importantly, they must be encouraged not to accept inferior workmanship coming from a previous work station. Because they rotate between stations, and thus are familiar with each step in the process, they are told to trust their own judgment. In this way, decision making is pushed down to the lowest level of the organization, following the same logic proposed in the price theory of why free market economies work.

The Director General conducts daily worker assemblies, where he personally reiterates his commitment to the policies being implemented, and seeks direct worker input about possible problems or improvements that workers may be able to identify in the process. His ability to speak Spanish increases the rapport he shares with his employees.

It is clear from each of these three steps that what is needed is individuals who will make decisions. As was seen in Chapter 3, however, Mexico ranks low on Hofstede's individualism criteria. Families, perhaps, take the place of individuals. Families function as the sources of a collective identity, and also serve as important sources of loyalty and pride. Within the family, the father has the final authority, just as the owner/director general, or *patrón,* has the final word within a company. By creating a team structure, with collective vs. individual identity, and giving each team the opportunity to develop self-pride via success in intergroup competitions, a parallel is created to the social structure with which Mexicans are familiar.

The crucial distinction between the family parallel and participatory teams is that the *patrón,* or the manager at any given level, must continue to maintain that absolute respect that his workers desire to accord to him, while simultaneously relinquishing enough authority to allow the team principles to succeed.

In his three years of managing in Mexico, the Director General always has been very impressed by the diligence, loyalty, and creativity of the Mexican worker. He describes them as extraordinarily cooperative, and willing to be of assistance within the company in any way that may be necessary, even if it be outside of their particular job description. "This positive work attitude, as well as taking pride in their work, has been stated by numerous managers of multinational plants operating in northern of Mexico."[3]

This company has successfully adapted the quality oriented team production method to Mexico's unique work culture, demonstrating its management's understanding of the needs to be aware of the cultural assumptions upon which any management scheme is based. By training the Mexican worker and management to accept empowerment, while capitalizing on the Mexican's loyalty and willingness to contribute, a valuable cultural synergy has been created. This Canadian company, its customers, and its employees all have benefitted from successful multicultural management, the type which will be necessary in order for companies to obtain optimal benefit from the opportunities that NAFTA offers them.

Case Three: Customer-Supplier Partnership and NAFTA[4]

When the NAFTA agreement was being negotiated, the Mexican government asked Mexican companies that had strong relationships with U.S. companies to ask those companies to work in support of the agreement by writing letters advocating ratification to their local congressional delegations.

Primarily due to the strong trust and business relationship built up over the years, CEMEX, one of the most successful international corporations in the cement industry, immediately contacted BHA Group Inc., a Kansas City based supplier that shared its commitment to service and responsiveness to customer needs, which are the hallmarks of the Total Quality Management (TQM) employed by both companies.

In the ensuing months, Luis Benavides, Corporate Purchasing Administration Manager of CEMEX, James J. Thome, Executive

---

[3] Boyce, James, E. and Thakur, Manub. "Participative Management in Mexico II," *Business Mexico*, September, 1986, p. 24.

[4] This case was written by Jeffrey D. Abbott with assistance and information supplied by Luis Benavides, James J. Thome and Michelle Jarnevic.

Vice President of BHA Group, Inc., and Michelle Jarnevic, BHA Group Manager of Corporate Training, worked together with uncompromising attention to promote support for the North American Free Trade Agreement.

Their communication was facilitated by the fact that Benavides had completed his graduate education in the United States, and therefore possessed not only a command of English, but also a familiarity with American culture that allowed him to establish personal relationships with his suppliers in the United States.

The American executive was also familiar with doing business in Mexico, as BHA Group Inc., an international supplier of replacement parts and services for air pollution control equipment, had been doing business in Mexico for over ten years. Mr. Thome had personally made countless trips to Latin America over the years and, as a result, had built a high level of trust and rapport with his Mexican counterparts.

BHA Group Inc. quickly went to work, starting a letter writing campaign by their employees, vendors, and stockholders. Over 75 letters went to their congressmen in Washington D.C. The company's vice chairman traveled to Washington D.C. on October 21, 1993, to attend a United States Chamber of Commerce Environmental Exports meeting held at the White House. Mr. Thome sent several editorial letters to the *Kansas City Star* newspaper, and he was able to persuade the Kansas City International Trade Club to publicly endorse NAFTA.

Indeed, these two companies felt so strongly about the value of their relationship, and about the even greater potential that it held under NAFTA, that both executives, with the blessing of both companies' highest management, decided to visit the congressional representatives several weeks before the ratification hearings.

BHA was able to set up three appointments, all of them with members of the House of Representatives, two from the district's in which BHA's corporate offices were located, and one with a member representing the district in which the company's manufacturing facility was situated. All three of the representatives were undecided on NAFTA at the time of the meeting. In fact, there was even a high degree of skepticism, as they feared that the low wages paid to Mexican workers would cost their districts valuable manufacturing jobs.

Mr. Benavides showed the congressmen that when all additional benefits are included in the base rate of pay, the disparity between wages in Mexico and the USA is by no means as alarming as has been reported. This very fact has been the source of many misconceptions about the true cost of doing business in Mexico. As a matter of fact, Mexican workers are entitled by law to receive benefits that many American and Canadian workers do not enjoy. Examples of these are:

- *Aguinaldo.* The mandatory Christmas bonus equivalent to a month's salary.
- *Profit sharing.* Exempt during their first year of operation, companies each year thereafter must pay 10 percent profit sharing to all employees, whether they be worker or manager.
- *Bonos.* Although not a legal requisite, a great majority of Mexican companies use this type of compensation, given its tax deductibility, as untaxed company paid benefits to workers. Bonos come in the form of coupons that are redeemable at food and general stores. The company may decide to pay a quantity of bonos equivalent to from 0–21 percent of base salary, but the rate paid must be a multiple of the minimum daily wage in the region.
- *Sistema de Ahorros Para el Retiro* (SAR). Companies must pay 2 percent of the employee's base rate of pay into this government mandated retirement savings program.
- *Fondo Ahorro.* An optional savings plan that companies may elect to provide for workers, in which case all workers must participate via payroll deductions. Workers must select a uniform rate of contribution. The company contributes an equal amount to that contributed by the worker.
- *Infonavit.* A government housing program that entitles every contributing worker to one day receiving a government built house, or all his/her money back plus interest.
- *I.M.S.S..* A comprehensive government system that provides healthcare and financial assistance to Mexican workers in the event of general sickness, involuntary termination, permanent

incapacitation, maternity (12 weeks) or sick leave, retirement, death, and/or childcare. There is also a recreational/social development program available to all members.

- *Paid Vacations.* All Mexican workers with at least one year of seniority are entitled to be paid one week of vacation at the rate of 25 percent of their daily base salary per day of vacation.
- *Involuntary Termination or Severance Pay.* By law, any Mexican worker who is involuntarily terminated is entitled to receive three months of severance pay plus twenty days extra per year worked.
- *Overtime.* Any time worked in addition to the regular 48 hour weekly schedule must be paid as overtime. The first nine hours are paid double, and all hours thereafter, or those worked during a national holiday, are paid triple. There are three minimum daily wage zones: 1) Mexico City; 2) Guadalajara & Monterrey; and 3) the rest of Mexico.

By law, Mexican employees also are entitled to one day off per week, but they must be paid their salary based upon seven working days per week. An employee who misses a day of work would therefore only lose 1/7 of the weekly salary.

Workers also receive their uniforms free, and frequently participate in group rate corporate health and automobile insurance programs. These benefits, which have been estimated by the U.S. consulting firm Hewitt and Associates to equal up to 62 percent of an industrial worker's base pay, had been largely ignored, and needed to be taken into account when discussing wage differentials. The congressional representatives were very receptive to this information.

In addition, Mr. Benavides, armed with official Mexican government statistics and information provided by SEDESOL (Mexico's equivalent of the Environmental Protection Agency) went on to show the efforts, in terms of funds, infrastructure, and development plans that Mexico has employed to clean up the environment, not only along the border, but throughout the rest of Mexico as well.

Whether or not it is attributable to the joint visit to Congress by CEMEX and BHA Group Inc., during the following week the three congressmen, equipped with more accurate information about the situation, announced their decision to vote in support of NAFTA.

These businesspeople and their companies continue to enjoy an unusually close and profitable business relationship founded upon a mutual appreciation of each other's countries, languages, and cultures. They knew that simply being well prepared and correctly informed was one of the most important factors in gathering the public support necessary to make NAFTA work.[5]

Case Four: Designing Market Penetrating Strategies for the Mexican Market[6]

The Commercial Group, Inc.'s (TCG's) main competitor in the U.S. OTC drug market decided to form a joint venture with a Mexico-based packaging firm. As TCG also had a potential interest in developing the Mexican market, they were justifiably concerned by this announcement. The details of the joint venture were reported in a local newspaper in Chicago, Illinois (the competitor's base), but the inexperienced reporter drafted the press release indicating that the purpose of this enterprise was only to subcontract the Mexican company's excess packaging capacity to supply the southwestern United States.

Desiring more concrete details about its competitor's new association, TCG hired a U.S. based intelligence consulting firm to investigate the activities of the Mexican partner, and to report on the expected benefits the joint venture would bring to their competitor.

Following the most common methodologies used in the U.S., the consulting firm designed their intelligence activities based 50 percent on secondary research and 50 percent on primary

---

[5] The authors recognize that while these benefits may technically be due Mexican workers, only a small percentage of workers actually receive them, notably, workers at the large industrial groups in Monterrey such as CEMEX. We should not overlook the many Mexican workers who toil at subsistence level wages without such benefits.

[6] Pedro Ortiz is president of IBDC, a market development consulting firm dealing primarily with Competitor's Intelligence activities, market research, and the design of market penetration strategies for international companies considering entry into the Mexican market.

research (primarily telephone interviews and the very rare face-to-face conversation). This methodology was made possible by the widespread availability of reliable secondary industry and market data in the USA, and in this case was necessary because of budgetary limitations imposed by TCG Group which did not allow more primary research to be done.

When the investigation was concluded, the reports were reviewed by TCG's Strategic Planning Department, which concluded that the joint venture did not pose a major threat to the group. The consultants concluded that the competition would only marginally increase its regional competitiveness in the southwest, by an amount that TCG could easily offset. Furthermore, they concluded that TCG's activities to develop the Mexican market would not be endangered.

Four months later, a state run Mexican conglomerate announced that its major subsidiary in the packaging industry was to be privatized, and that the new owner would be a recently formed joint venture between a Mexican packaging company and a U.S. firm. The combined strength of the new company would give it 63 percent of the OTC drugs market in the rural areas of Mexico, an underdeveloped market of 42 million consumers with an annual growth potential of 11 percent. TCG wondered what had happened.

At the time the joint venture was first announced, a TCG executive made some calls and managed to confirm that the joint venture was indeed to be a reality, and that it was true that some of the competitor's southwestern packaging needs would be met by subcontracting from the Mexican partner. He did not, however, pursue the issue further to find out if these new packaging needs included those that would be necessary to cover the Mexican OTC drug market.

Thinking only in terms of "saving money" on consulting activities, TCG stated its intelligence objectives very narrowly, focusing only on the potential impact in U.S. markets of the subcontracted packaging activities. As a result, the consulting firm had only revised the Mexican Department of Commerce's statistics corresponding to the type of packaging material in question, but the product codes employed in Mexico were not as specific as those used in the U.S. The research was misguided, believing that there was a significant unidirectional volume of product crossing the border into the United States, which caused TCG to assume that the competitor was not making inroads into Mexico.

Recently, the Mexican Secretary of Commerce has made an immense effort to improve the accuracy and coverage of such statistics, but unfortunately these efforts were not of assistance to TCG at the time of this incident.

In Mexico, personal relationships are very important. Telephone interviews are not common nor are they very welcomed. In the specific cases that telephone interviews need to be conducted, the desire of Mexicans to be courteous and to avoid conflict may cause the interviewee to merely "go along" with the interviewer, thereby communicating, with no harmful intentions, misleading information with poor meaning content. Notwithstanding the improvements that have occurred in the collection of secondary market data in Mexico, competitor's intelligence activities always should be carried out with a local Mexican partner who knows the cultural dimension of these activities.

Case Five: Vitro/Whirlpool A Transformation of Organizational Culture[7]

One of the best known joint ventures between a Mexican and American company is that formed in 1987 by Vitro and Whirlpool in the household appliance industry. Vitro, Mexico's largest private company and the nation's number one glass maker, has 51 percent of the venture, while Whirlpool, an international leader in the household appliance industry, has 49 percent. Together, they design, manufacture, and market household appliances for Mexico, Latin America, and the U.S.

In 1992, both companies implemented Total Quality Programs. Whirlpool's quality system, known as its "Worldwide Excellence System (WES)," had been implemented in the U.S. in 1990. Vitro's system, "The Ing. Adrian Sada Treviño Total Quality

---

[7] This case was written by Jeffrey D. Abbott and Fernando Fernandez, vice president of Quality and Procurement in Vitro's Household Products Division located in Monterrey, Mexico, where Whirlpool is a joint venture partner.

System," is named after the firm's chairman, and was implemented in 1991.

As they had begun a year earlier, Whirlpool suggested at one point that Vitro might try its WES system, and sent a veteran company quality expert to help with its implementation. Perhaps believing in the superiority of their system and American know-how, they simply tried to transplant WES. This was not done forcefully, rather offered as a suggestion of something that might work for Vitro. Spanish translations were made available, but Whirlpool did not undertake the critical process of self-evaluation to determine if WES could function effectively as it was, or if it would be necessary to adapt it in some way to Vitro's management and its Mexican workers. This initial experience was a classic example of the management ethnocentrism that often plagued U.S.-Mexican operations, but today's results can serve as an impressive example of corporate and cultural synergy, achieved through cultural sensitivity and the just respect for and integration of two cultural management styles.

To effect the transformation to a quality mentality, organizational excellence processes were put into place to define the gradual pace that change would take along the path to achieving the goals set forth in the TQ systems. Some differences existed in both companies' quality programs, but the difficulties the two companies encountered stemmed from the larger differences between the processes that would be used to implement them. Figure 5-2 shows the two processes, AST and WES, as well as QUEST, the hybrid that was made when they were synergized by the joint venture: Vitro, due to Mexico's previously closed economy, long had been manufacturing oriented, and had a strongly centralized authoritarian management culture in which considerable influence from the controlling family was felt. Whirlpool's culture was described by Ralph Hake, President of its North American Appliance Group, as one where people work hard, play hard, and share an intensity in their common pursuit of customer satisfaction. Both companies have enjoyed noteworthy success.

Perhaps the hardest companies to try to change, however, are those that have been successful. This is especially true when those

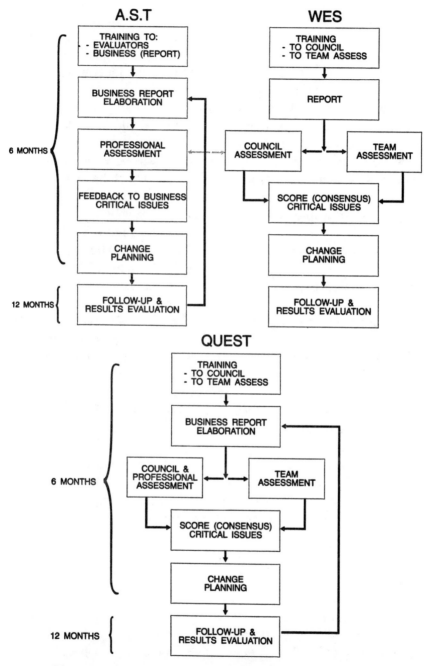

Figure 5-2. *Organizational Excellence Processes.*

same companies undertake international expansion, and assume that their proven practices from their home country may simply be transferred to the host country. Failure to consider the need to adapt their processes and management to the local work culture can result in frustration and false starts.

Whirlpool skipped the critical process of helping to create within Vitro and its employees the vision of what could be achieved via Total Quality. Whirlpool did not go far enough in explaining the "por que" to the Mexicans, that is, why change was necessary and what benefits would come from change. Mexicans have a unique management and work culture, and are especially sensitive to the imposition of a foreign way, especially if that way is American.

The one-year quality cycle diagrammed in Figure 5-2 has been completed three times now at Vitro/Whirlpool. After the second year, there was evidence of only a gradual change. More needed to be done to explain the benefits of the new system to the workers, to give them an incentive to push it forward.

Figure 5-3 was designed by Vitro for use at all levels as a tool for helping to focus the discussion. At the time of its introduction, Vitro already had defined the vision and possessed the skills, but still needed a way to help employees visualize where they had come from and where they were going.

From the experiences these companies have had in managing change since 1987, both have learned valuable lessons about the stages at which American involvement in a process of change can be helpful and indeed essential, and at what points Mexicans must be left to their own devices to achieve it. In accordance with the variables presented above, the following are suggestions about intercultural change management based on the experience of Vitro and Whirlpool.

Vision

Definition. During this stage, transformation managers must create a vision for the desired future state of the company. The origination of such a process does not come so naturally to Mexicans, and Vitro found that Americans and the specialized knowledge they bring was very helpful at this stage. Even before

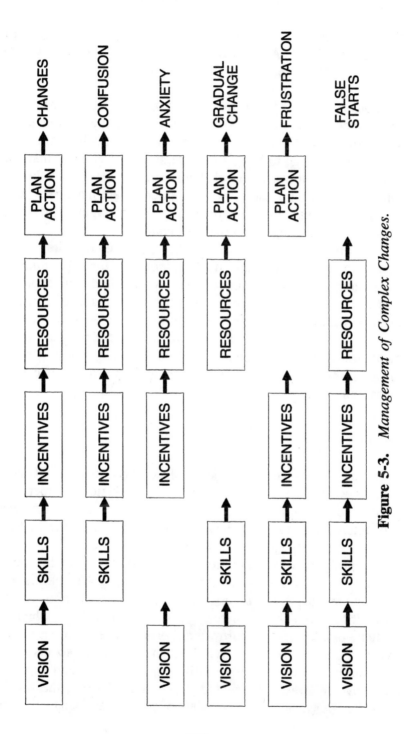

Figure 5-3. *Management of Complex Changes.*

the joint venture had begun with Whirlpool, Vitro enlisted the assistance of the American Production and Quality Center (APQC) in Houston, Texas.

Implementation. The Mexican transformation management team must understand what has been defined in the Vision stage. Therefore, APQC "change agents" were again brought in to spread the message to Vitro's managers. Any resentment that may have been felt towards the changes being made would thus be directed at them, instead of at Vitro's permanent managers. After the process was explained to Vitro's managers, however, Mexicans were integrally involved again.

Two Mexican leaders, to be known as "evaluators," were trained in each division and made responsible for explaining the TQ system to the rest of the workers. A "trickle down" approach was used: senior managers spoke to middle managers, middle managers to line managers, and they to the workers, but always in small intimate groups, carefully reviewing the program documentation and requirements. Mexicans naturally respond better to Mexicans; therefore they must explain this process of change to one another.

Skills

To take advantage of their specialized knowledge, APQC consultants were invited to further train the evaluators—Americans were used to train the trainers. A double cultural barrier was encountered at this point, however, that obstructed the method of fact-based management that they were instructing.

The problem was encountered in the first step at the point where team assessments are conducted. First, given the historic lack of emphasis placed on record keeping in Mexico, it was difficult to establish objective, fact-based criteria upon which to evaluate employee or departmental performance. Without objective criteria, highly sensitive Mexicans are likely to take any criticism personally. Their sensitivity is reinforced and substantiated by the second element of the cultural barrier, the highly authoritarian Mexican management style. Mexican managers have traditionally had great power and autonomy, resulting in the acceptability and prevalence of more subjective evaluations of employees. Managers are reluctant to change if it means giving up their power, and thus they may even work against data gathering and the establishment of objective evaluative criteria. They are especially reluctant to change if their more participation-minded American neighbors are suggesting such changes. Therefore, Mexicans were again required to undertake the implementation of these ideas themselves.

Mexican people are very sensitive, and they find it difficult to separate people from problems. Criticism is frequently taken personally, making what Americans consider objective, constructive criticism a more delicate subject to address. In a high power-distance society such as Mexico, the boss traditionally has not needed a set of objective evaluative criteria to defend his judgments. Neither has a high premium been placed upon planning and documentation until recently. Some principles needed to be established to regulate the dialogue of change. Mexicans, opening themselves to criticism, need some assurance about the categories into which such criticism could fall.

What happened unknowingly followed the concepts of "principled negotiation." As Roger Fisher and William Ury note in *Getting to Yes*, "principled negotiation suggests that you look for mutual gains whenever possible, and that where your interests conflict, you should insist that the results be based upon some fair standards independent of the will of the other side. The method of principled negotiation is hard on merits, soft on people."[8]

Incentives

In this stage, the average worker's question of "what's in it for me?" must be addressed, but the worker also must believe in his ability to make a valuable contribution. Fernando Fernandez, Quality Leader at Vitro, believes for one to be able to give his/her best to the organization, which the commitment to quality requires, one must first see something of value within oneself.

---

[8] Fisher, R. and Ury, W. *Getting to Yes.* Boston: Houghton Mifflin, 1981.

For that reason, he employs a four-step self-motivation program with his employees.

Step One: **Attitude.** Helping develop the employee's belief that he/she is valuable and can contribute to progress.

Step Two: **Learn.** People like to learn, especially if they believe that their managers are interested in their progress.

Step Three: **Apply.** Workers can see for themselves, via application, that the learned concepts are useful.

Step Four: **Recognition.** Informal recognition can be given through personal recognition, plaques for achievement, etc.

Formal recognition can be given through group awards to the best performing division, and salary bonuses can be given to individuals that are paid through a variable compensation plan that takes into account scores in the AST Quality Program evaluations.

AST Vitro Award. Recognition is given for the best division and most improved division.

Resources

Having established objective criteria for evaluating progress and provided managers with an incentive to "buy-in" to the system, senior managers already committed to the TQ system must be helped by change agents to visualize the specific results they could achieve by fully committing available resources to the plan.

Directors who aren't well-trained in the system, who do not believe in the vision, will not want to invest in it; rather they will tend to think of it as an "expense." Transformation managers must therefore "sell" the program to their superiors, presenting it as an investment as opposed to an expense. (Quieren hacer todo con las uñas.) In Mexico it may be necessary to invest more in employee training due to the lower average level of education of the Mexican worker.

Action

Leaders must work together to decide where, when, and how the changes will be effected, and by whom. It is of extreme importance to have the discipline to follow the plan step by step as it has been designed, although it is a Mexican tendency to shoot from the hip. (Tirar sin apuntar).

Although it has not traditionally been a Mexican priority, one way to help keep on plan is to document everything thoroughly. In this way, there is no question from whence you have come and to where you are going. Documentation also reduces the company's dependence upon individuals, by recording their knowledge so that it is not lost when they leave the company. Documenting is one of the most important things individuals can do to ensure that the quality program and cultural transformation succeeds.

Conclusion

Catalyzing organizational change and creating synergy between two organizations is difficult. When divergent cultural variables are added to the equation, such as those that exist between the U.S. and Mexico, an entirely different set of challenges are confronted.

In many ways a joint venture is like a negotiation: participants can work against one another by insisting on clinging to established ways, or can pursue mutual interests and utilize each party's competencies to create a new and profitable synergy. The process is much more involved than simply combining or sharing technology. Workers and managers from both companies must learn to interact effectively and in a manner that accords the respect deserved to both companies' established way of doing things, while simultaneously allowing for transformation and synergy to take place.

Ethnocentrism hinders individuals performance internationally, and "corporocentrism," if you will, the belief that your company's way of doing things is inherently better in all respects, is an equally damaging attitude in a strategic partnership. Vitro and Whirlpool have learned to work together, technologically and interculturally. The synergistic management they have developed is one important reason for the success they enjoy as partners.

Case Six: Opening the Canadian Market[9]

During the Second World War, when U.S. brewers stopped producing, Americans first became familiar with the excellent Mexican beers brewed at the Cerveceria Cuahutémoc, Mexico's largest brewery. Since that time, its well known brands, such as Tecate, Dos Equis, Bohemia, and Carta Blanca have become familiar words to beer drinkers.

As is often the case for companies entering foreign markets, the Cerveceria had already made some changes to its products to market them successfully in the United States. Americans, for example, are accustomed to drinking beer in 12-ounce bottles, a slightly larger bottle than those used in Mexico; and where Mexicans prefer returnable glass bottles, the American consumer prefers them to be disposable.

On a superficial level, it may appear that the Canadian and American markets are identical, and that whatever works in the United States will function equally well in Canada. This is an assumption that many Americans make. As Juan Garcia-Sordo, then director of International Sales for the Cerveceria discovered, Canada has its own proud history, culture, and unique market, which are distinct from their American counterparts.

In Canada, alcohol sales are confined to government stores, and the government maintains the sole right to determine which products may be imported into the country. The market is much more tightly controlled than in either Mexico or the U.S., resulting in differences in distribution and marketing strategies. In contrast to the tight control in Canada, small "mom and pop" stores are important distribution points for end-consumer products in Mexico, and marketers have great latitude in promotional activities in these stores.

---

[9] This case was written by Jeffrey D. Abbott, based on information provided by Juan Garcia-Sordo, director of the Department of International Business at the Instituto Teconologico y de Estudios Superiores de Monterrey, and former manager of international sales at the Cerveceria Cuahutémoc.

For alcoholic beverages to be sold in Canada, they must be submitted to government testing, a process that usually takes 6–12 months, but could take five years. This complicated process would be easily understood and managed by a local Canadian distributor who was familiar with it. Garcia-Sordo's first decision was to seek a local partner.

To facilitate the process of product approval, the local partner needed to be a person with a good relationship with the government testing agency. The government wanted to be assured that the product would be excellent, and that the beer would be represented by a respected member of the local business community.

In the government controlled liquor stores, no publicity or point of purchase advertising is allowed. Additionally, in Canada, as in many countries, restrictions exist about the nature of television advertising. With such restricted promotional opportunities, foreign marketers, unfamiliar with local customers and markets, could lose time and dollars optimally promoting the product in another culture.

Over time, Garcia-Sordo cemented what was already a strong and trusting business relationship with his Canadian counterparts. A common feature of Mexican and Canadian cultures that distinguish both countries from the United States, is the importance of family ties and relationship building.

Canadian management style reflects a British influence, which is somewhere between the hard-driving directness of the American and the more reserved style of the British. Mexicans, Canadians, and Americans cannot lose sight of the fact that culture will determine a country's unique market.

References

1. Statland de Lopez, R., "Moving to Mexico," *Business Mexico,* May 1992, p. 46.
2. Kras, E., "Cultural Awareness Pays in Mexican Workplace," *Business Mexico,* August 1986.
3. Statland de Lopez, R., "Moving to Mexico," *Business Mexico,* May 1992, p. 46.

Canadian, American, and Mexican Negotiating Profiles

Presidential candidate H. Ross Perot was a vigorous foe of NAFTA. During his many television appearances, not lacking an opinion about anything, he articulated views on a variety of topics, including the Mexican people. Perot's opinions were prejudicial, reflected his own stereotypes, and inaccurately characterized large numbers of Mexicans. All but Perot's most ardent supporters recognized his myopic, biased views.

Stereotypes

Profiles of Canadian, American, and Mexican negotiators appear in the second part of this chapter. We believe the profiles are accurate reflections of national character and do not contain stereotypes. The profiles do not apply to every individual Canadian, Mexican, or American, but they apply to most. Stereotypes, on the other hand, apply to a few people in the culture and are attributed to most. Perhaps this fictitious visit of an individual to a therapist will illustrate this point. An individual was sent to see a psychiatrist because he believed he was dead. "Do dead men bleed?" asked the doctor. The patient said, "Of course not." The psychiatrist then jabbed him in the arm with a needle. At first puzzled and then disappointed, the man saw blood ooze out of his arm. Then his face brightened, he regained his composure and said, "Well imagine that, dead men do bleed."

The person who thought he was dead was thinking and reacting according to his preconception of reality. He made reality fit his perception.

The word stereotype did not occur in the English language until 1922 when Walter Lippmann first used it in his book, *Public Opinion.* Lippmann believed that stereotypes organize images, are fixed and simplified, and certain features are chosen to stand for the whole. Lippmann also stated that stereotypes are defense mechanisms, and are essentially incorrect, inaccurate, and therefore undesirable.

The authors believe that most individuals use stereotyping when first meeting someone. Our first impressions of a person often are based on the stereotypes we have formulated. Stereotypes serve the purpose of reducing ambiguities in one's view of reality. *The danger is that most stereotypes are partially errone-ous,* and the unvarying patterns they engender may not apply.

Many years ago Lippmann wrote [1]:

> ... the accounts of returning travellers are often an interesting tale of what the traveller carried abroad with him on his trip. If he carried chiefly his appetite, a zeal for tiled bathrooms, a conviction that the Pullman car is the acme of human comfort, and a belief that it is proper to tip waiters, taxicab drivers, and barbers, but under no circumstances station agents and ushers, then his odyssey will be replete with good meals and bad meals, bathing adventures, compartment-train escapades, and voracious demands for money. Or if he is a more serious soul he may while on tour have found himself at celebrated spots. Having touched base, and cast one furtive glance at the monument, he buried his head in Baedeker, read every word through, and moved on to the next celebrated spot; and thus returned with a compact and orderly impression of Europe, rated one star or two.

Figure 6-1 suggests some of the factors that might influence the development of stereotypes.

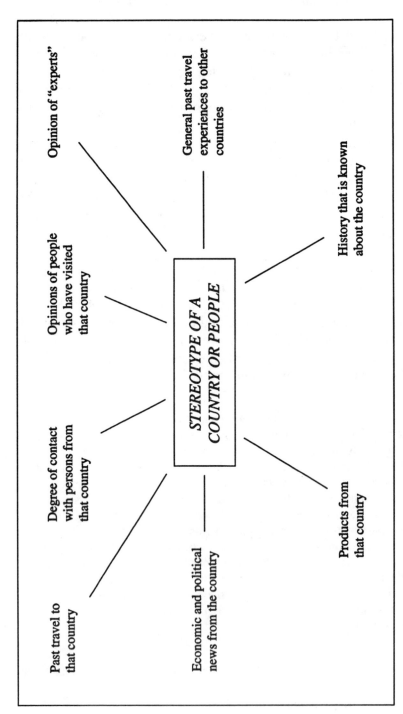

Figure 6-1. *Factors That Influence the Development of Stereotypes.*

The Concept of National Character

Edward Hall [2], the famous anthropologist wrote, "Culture hides much more than it reveals, and strangely enough what it hides, it hides most effectively from its own participants."

The concept of "national character," or a pattern of common attitudes, values, and beliefs shared by a culture was developed by Dr. Abram Kardiner and Dr. Ralph Linton [3]. The concept rests on the following premises:

1. That an individual's early experiences exert a lasting effect.
2. That similar early experiences tend to produce similar personality profiles in the people who experience them.
3. That the child-rearing practices and socialization techniques of a society are culturally patterned and tend to be similar (although not identical) for the various families within the culture.
4. That these practices and techniques differ from culture to culture.

A wealth of evidence has been provided by anthropologists, sociologists, psychologists, and others to support these premises and it follows that:

1. Members of any culture have many elements of early experience in common.
2. They also have many elements of personality in common.
3. Since the early experience of individuals differs from one culture to another, the personality characteristics and values differ from culture to culture.

The national character of a society is the personality configuration shared by most members of the culture, as a result of early experiences they have in common. Obviously, this does not mean that the behavior patterns of all members of a culture are similar. There is a wide range of individual differences, but there are many aspects that most of the people share to varying degrees.

Edward T. Hall stated it this way [4]:

Deep cultural undercurrents structure life in subtle but highly consistent ways that are not consciously formulated. Like the invisible jet streams in the skies that determine the course of a storm, these hidden currents shape our lives; yet their influence is only beginning to be identified.

A Framework for Negotiating

A respected colleague, William J. Stripp [5], developed a framework for profiling one's negotiating counterparts. According to Stripp, negotiation is a process involving policy formulation, the interaction of the negotiators, deliberation of the issues, and an outcome.

Hypothetically, company A from the United States wants to negotiate an alliance with company B from Mexico. Stripp explains:

> In preparing for the negotiations, A wants to answer the following questions about B: **Policy**—What is B's philosophy of negotiation? How does B choose its negotiators? What does B want? How will the negotiators act? **Interaction**—How will B's negotiators try to persuade us? What forms of nonverbal communication will be used? How will B's negotiators organize time? **Deliberation**—How can we get B's negotiators to trust us? Are they willing to take risks? On what will they base their decisions? **Outcome**—How can we reach an agreement?
>
> "Policy" defines the vital interests of a business and describes the customary course of action used to protect and promote those interests. In world trade and investment, businesses have three broad policy alternatives: isolation in the domestic market, competition on a global scale, or cooperation in the creation of strategic alliances. All three choices require cross-cultural negotiation.
>
> "Interaction" is the period of information exchange during which the negotiators propose offers and counteroffers. The process of interaction is a continual stream of acts, words and gestures that are intended to persuade the counterpart. The flow of information permits each party to learn about the counterpart's expectations.
>
> 'Deliberation' is the process by which the negotiators evaluate interaction, adjust their understanding of the counterpart's requirements, and reformulate expectations, preferences and proposals in an effort to resolve conflicting interest.
>
> 'Outcome' refers to the final understanding reached by the parties. The negotiators may come to some agreement or may conclude that agreement is impossible.

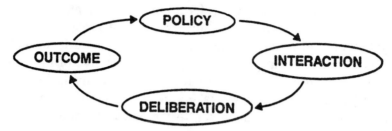

Figure 6-2. *Global Negotiations Flowchart.*

Profile of Canadian Negotiators[1]

"There is no Canadian story. There are English-Canadian stories, French-Canadian stories . . . [6]"

There are two dominant cultural groups in Canada. Each of these groups has a 'typical' negotiating style. The English Canadian culture is the dominant group in the provinces of Ontario, British Columbia, Alberta, Manitoba, Saskatchewan, Nova Scotia, New Brunswick, Newfoundland and Prince Edward Island. There is also a strong English Canadian minority in the province of Quebec mainly centered in Montreal. The French Canadian culture is dominant in Quebec where the official language of the province is French. There is a strong French Canadian minority in New Brunswick and also in eastern Ontario around the national capital city of Ottawa.

Basic Concept of Negotiation

English and French Canadians tend to confront conflict and focus on points of disagreement as they work through a linear problem solving process. This process involves identifying the problem or opportunity, the objectives of the negotiation, the alternatives, the decision, and the plan for action. English Canadians tend to focus on abstract or theoretical values and less on practical facts or key issues that have come out of the negotiation process.

---

[1] The profile of Canadian negotiators was written by Neil R. Abramson, Ph.D. Assistant Professor of International Business, Faculty of Business Administration, Simon Fraser University, Burnaby, British Columbia, Canada.

French Canadians tend to prefer a more instrumental and individualistic approach to negotiating. The goal of French Canadian negotiators is to influence the other party, and there is a greater concern with achieving one's own goals irrespective of the goals of the other side. They tend to focus on relationship building during non-task activities but take a more aggressive, controversial, and argumentative approach to the actual negotiations.

Selection of Negotiators

English and French Canadian negotiators usually are chosen for a negotiating team based on their knowledge, expertise, and previous experience concluding successful negotiations. In technical negotiations, technical experts may be brought in to present complex information. Individual differences such as gender, age, and social class are less important for English than French Canadians. The latter tend to accept greater levels of inequality and ability between different levels of management and are more likely not to send any negotiators if the situation precludes their ability to achieve their individual objectives.

Role of Individual Aspirations

Canadian culture encourages individual aspirations and achievement. Most Canadians are expected to represent the objectives of their organizations ahead of their personal objectives.

English Canadians, however, believe that it is in their self interest to adopt cooperative bargaining strategies to achieve cooperation from their counterparts. French Canadians believe that it is in their self interest to use more competitive strategies because cooperation does not elicit mutual cooperation in Quebec.

Concern with Protocol

English and French Canadians tend to be at least superficially friendly and informal. English Canadians are less concerned with protocol and usually commence their business with very few preliminaries. They tend to be organized in firms with relatively flat hierarchies, and superiors mix and interact freely with subordinates. French Canadians are more concerned with protocol and ceremony. They do tend to recognize the authority and additional responsibility of superiors.

Significance of Type of Issue

English Canadians are dedicated to the goal of getting the job done. They seem even less concerned than Americans with building and developing relationships, and are both impersonal and task oriented, as are the French Canadians.

Complexity of Language

English Canadians, like their American neighbors, are low-context communicators. The message sent by the words spoken are the intended messages. French-speaking Canadians are high context communicators, because the spoken word is only one part of the total message.

Canadians have been described as being "relentlessly polite." Canadians often do not communicate their expectations clearly because it might be perceived as impolite. Canadians, however, are adept at picking up these signals. A Canadian negotiator might 'suggest,' 'hope,' 'think' or 'wish,' and this may be intended as a strong statement of expectation. Canadians may not complain openly about the negotiating process, but if their signals are ignored, they may become less conciliatory and cooperative. Canadians often do not give clear instructions to subordinates or negotiation counterparts, but within Canadian management culture, the instructions are clear and one is expected to execute them.

Nature of Persuasive Argument

Canadians use a rational presentation style with detailed facts and figures organized to support a clearly stated position. A deductive style is favored when parties are expected to be in agreement. This style presents the key recommendations first, followed by the key supporting information. An inductive style is preferred when persuasion is necessary. In this case, supporting information is presented first then builds toward acceptance of an argument that is presented last.

Value of Time

English and French Canadians tend to be rigidly bound by their schedules and deadlines. Promptness both beginning and ending meetings is appreciated. If one is made to wait more than five or ten minutes for a scheduled interview, many Canadian business people assume that a personal slight is intended.

English Canadians are significantly slower in their use of time than Americans are because of their cooperative bargaining approach and their constructive approach to controversy and conflict handling. They prefer to delay decision making in favor of gathering more information, often to the frustration of their counterparts.

Bases of Trust

Canadian managers seem to believe that trust is an important component in achieving organizational and inter-organizational goals. They believe this even when dealing with negotiators from cultures where trust is not a competitive advantage or may even be a competitive liability.

English Canadians tend to trust the information that is being communicated as long as their counterpart uses a cooperative negotiating strategy that emphasizes the free exchange of information. An agreement will result in a contract that can be enforced legally. If, however, English Canadian negotiators perceive that their counterparts are not using a cooperative strategy, then trust is damaged because the counterpart may seem to be more interested in achieving individual outcomes rather than joint outcomes.

French Canadians may tend to distrust information more than English Canadians do. French Canadians tend to use more competitive negotiation strategies that place individual objectives ahead of joint outcomes. These strategies are used even though their use lowers satisfaction with the negotiating process. If two parties are competing for advantage, misinformation could provide an advantage if it was believed by the other party. There is no advantage in providing correct information that helps a counterpart have a clearer idea of the situation.

Profile of American Negotiators

Basic Concept of Negotiation

American negotiators view conflict and confrontation as an opportunity to exchange viewpoints and as part of the process in resolution, negotiation, and agreement. Americans prefer outlining the issues or problems and a direct approach to determining possible solutions. They are motivated to further the interests of their corporation or government and have a highly competitive nature regarding the outcome or settlement. Americans respect their counterparts, but can take an attitude that "this is business" and set relationships aside to reach agreement.

Selection of Negotiators

American negotiators usually are chosen for a negotiating team based on their record of success in past negotiations and their knowledge and expertise in the area to be negotiated. Negotiations that are technical in nature require Americans with very specific knowledge and the ability to communicate their expertise. Individual differences, sex, age, and social class are not generally criteria for selection, but individual differences in character (cooperative, authoritarian, trustworthy) can determine whether one is chosen for an American negotiating team.

Role of Individual Aspirations

As a rule, Americans encourage individual aspirations and individual achievements. When representing her/his corporation or country, Americans temper their individualism and seek to accomplish and or represent the positions of their company or country.

Concern with Protocol

Generally, Americans are friendly and open. Their etiquette is largely informal and so is their basic concern for protocol. They are relaxed in their business conduct and often do not adhere to strict or explicit codes of behavior and ceremony. They do recognize the authority and responsibility of superiors, but still feel, in most cases, that superiors are approachable.

Significance of Type of Issue

The American popular expression of "getting the job done" reflects their desire to assess the situation and get results quickly. In negotiations, Americans may focus on the tangible aspects of the negotiation without spending too much time on such intangible aspects as building relationships during the process. They want to reach an agreement that satisfies the tangible interests of the negotiation.

Complexity of Language

Edward T. Hall compares low context communication with interfacing with a computer. The communication is done through a system of explicit exchanges via prompts and responses, and if an inaccurate response is not within the realm of the computer's programming then "it does not compute." Americans are low context communicators. The message is primarily in the words spoken and is not overridden by nonverbal cues, such as gestures, eye contact, and silence. Many cultures are high context communicators where much information is transmitted through the shared experiences and meanings of the culture and language, and the person speaking. English speaking Canada is also low context, while French speaking Canada and Mexico are high context.

Nature of Persuasive Argument

Americans' use of a rational presentation with detailed facts and figures accompanied by logical and analytical arguments is usually the course attempted when persuading one's counterparts.

Value of Time

Every culture has different ways of organizing time and using it. Some cultures are rigidly bound by their schedules and meeting deadlines, while other cultures have a relaxed attitude about detailed plans and schedules. Monochronic time emphasizes schedules, segmentation, and promptness. Polychronic time stresses involvement with people and completion of transactions rather than an adherence to a pre-set schedule. Americans generally have a monochronic time orientation, and for most Americans "time is money." In negotiations, Americans set schedules and appointments and tend to priortize events and move through the process "controlling" the time allotted them.

Bases of Trust

In negotiations, Americans generally trust the information being communicated and negotiated is accurate, and they assume that the negotiations will have a desirable outcome. If, however, Americans have had a past experience with a counterpart who has not been trustworthy, they will withhold the trust. Americans are also more comfortable with legal counsel advising them during the process.

Risk Taking Propensity

Americans are risk takers. In light of their history, their perception of their rugged individualism, and the rewards of capitalism, Americans have embraced risk and are not risk avoidant.

Internal Decision Making Systems

Decision making is becoming more and more decentralized with authority, within pre-determined limits, being given to those with negotiating experience; however, most of the final decisions must be cleared with senior executives in the organization.

Form of Satisfactory Agreement

Because the American culture is legalistic, Americans prefer and expect detailed contractual agreements to formalize negotiations. A handshake may conclude negotiations, but the attorneys representing both sides will hammer out the legal implications of the agreement.

Profile of Mexican Negotiators [7]

Basic Concept of Negotiation Process

Negotiating in Mexico is a complex and long procedure, covering several stages. First, the parties involved must determine if they, as individuals or organizations, can do business together. Establishing a warm working relationship with one's counterparts is essential to the process, and facilitates the negotiation.

At the negotiation table, because of past historical context, a Mexican negotiator is wary of being taken advantage of by an American *gringo*. The Mexican *machismo* (pride) will not allow this to happen. It is important for a negotiator to be sensitive to any real or implied messages regarding Mexican self-esteem.

Connections in Mexico are very important and the government has a significant influence in private business matters. Permits are required for just about every business transaction. As a result, a government official might elicit a bit of *mordida* (the bite) to complete the transaction.

Selection of Negotiators

Negotiators are selected primarily on status. Family connections, personal or political influence, and education are critical.

Hence the importance of *ubicacion* (where one is plugged into the system) becomes evident. Mexican negotiators tend to be high level, male, and well-connected.

Role of Individual Aspirations

Whether Mexicans are individualists or collectivists seems to depend on the social arena. In business, and with other men, Mexicans tend to be competitive, set on pursuing individual goals and needs for their personal recognition. Often they feel they owe loyalty to their *patron,* but they seek to project a public image of significance and power.

Concern for Protocol

Mexican culture is dominated by courtesy, dignity, tact, and diplomacy. Protocol is important and social competence is as critical as technical competence.

Significance of Type of Issue

For Mexicans, relationship-based and personal/internal issues tend to predominate and affect the negotiations, and Mexicans emphasize the social and personal aspects of their relationships with the people they encounter, including businessmen.

Many Mexicans resent what they see as a long history of unfair treatment by the North Americans, and personal honor or dignity may be a factor within the Mexican negotiating team.

Complexity of the Language

Communicative context is formed by body language and emotional cues, not just the words spoken. Mexicans communicate with hand movements, physical contact, and emotional expressions, making Mexicans high context communicators.

All Latin American cultures embrace closeness. People stand close to each other, sit close to each other, and often touch each other.

Nature of Persuasive Argument

Emotional arguments that are overly dramatic and patriotic are considered persuasive. Along these lines, there is the concept of *proyectismo* (constructing plans without critical analysis and assuming in time all will be accomplished). Perhaps much of this stems from the twin origins of Mexican culture: the Indian, based on magic and superstition, and the Spanish, based on imposition, dogma, and faith.

Value of Time

There is a relaxed polychronic attitude toward time. Although time is a concern, Mexicans do not allow schedules to interfere with experiences involving their family or friends. The culture is more people- rather than task-oriented.

Bases of Trust

Evaluations of trustworthiness are based initially on intuition and then later on one's past record. Negotiations should take place within a generally trusting atmosphere. Trust must develop through a series of frequent and warm interpersonal transactions, either socially or through business.

Risk Taking Propensity

Mexicans tend to be risk-avoidant. They will try to work something out to avoid risk as much as possible. Mexicans tend to be pessimistic in any situation in which there is some amount of risk.

Internal Decision Making System

Decision making is highly centralized in government, companies, and within negotiating teams. Mexican leaders tend to make decisions without concern for consensus. Individuals with *palanca* (leverage) tend to be well positioned, expressive, and forceful with their opinions and decisions.

Form of Satisfactory Agreement

The only way to be certain that a business agreement has been reached in Mexico is with a written document. Agreements in Mexico fall under the Civil Code, the Commercial Code, or the Law of Commercial Companies.

Conclusion

We began this chapter with a caution about stereotyping and recommended, instead, trying to understand the national character Canadians, Mexicans, and Americans might exhibit when negotiating.

However, not every Canadian, American, or Mexican negotiator fits the profiles perfectly; obviously there are important individual differences. Also the context of the negotiation, where it takes place, any previous relationships between negotiators, and the corporate and or government history, etc., all factor into the process and individualize each negotiation. The profiles are intended to be starting points to generate understanding and respect for the counterparts' cultural background and history, and optimally to create mutually beneficial business relationships.

References

1. Lippmann, W., *Public Opinion,* New York: Macmillan, 1922.
2. Hall, E.T., *The Silent Language,* Garden City, New York: Anchor Press, 1973.
3. Harris, P.R. and Moran, R.T., *Managing Cultural Differences,* Third Edition, Houston, TX: Gulf Publishing Co., 1991. (From Kardiner A. and Linton R., *The Psychological Frontiers of Society,* Westport, CT: Greenwood Press, 1981.)
4. Hall, E.T., *Beyond Culture,* Garden City, NY: Anchor Press, 1977.

5. Moran, R.T. and Stripp, W.G., *Successful International Business Negotiations,* Houston, TX: Gulf Publishing Co., 1991.
6. Cruickshank, J., "Canada's Search for Identity," *The Christian Science Monitor,* February 26, 1992.
7. Moran, R.T. and Stripp, W.G., *Successful International Business Negotiations,* Houston, TX: Gulf Publishing Co., 1991.

Competencies Required to Work Effectively Together

As readers of this book well realize, many global business projects fail because persons from different cultures have difficulties working together.

What factors contribute to the success of global projects? Some of the factors can be found in organizational structure, the vision of the company, as well as the strategies used to implement corporate vision. However, much of the success or failure of any global project can be attributed to the competencies of the individuals involved.

Working Globally

Persons working in a global environment first must learn to be less ethnocentric. How can people communicate if they judge each other's cultural customs as foolish, ridiculous, or not quite as good as their own? Skillful international managers have learned to see the world differently and understand the way others manage and do business. This implies that there is no. single way of doing anything and that no one has the best of everything.

Some of the material from the following section is drawn from *Managing Cultural Differences,* Third Edition, Gulf Publishing Company, and columns on cross-cultural contact published in *International Management.* Used with permission.

Many persons feel comfortable in predictable environments. Successful global managers, however, are able to react to new, different, and unpredictable situations with little visible discomfort or irritation.

Discomfort leads to frustration and negative feelings that discourage positive relationships with business partners from other cultures. Witness any U.S. business person in Mexico who is trying to accomplish tasks quickly and directly and is greeted by responses indicating delays.

Skillful global managers have a wide range of alternatives available to solve each dilemma and to know the implications of each in different cultures or business systems. In short, they are good problem solvers.

Global managers must learn how to do business with each other. The following illustrates this point. With a group of Americans and a group of Mexicans, researchers used a medical instrument that tests vision. On one side of the instrument they had a 35mm slide taken during a bullfight. On the other side, they had a slide taken during a baseball game. For less than a second, the bullfight and the baseball game slide had light projected behind them. The psychologist asked the Americans and the Mexicans one question: "What did you see?"

Most Americans said, "I saw the baseball game." Most Mexicans said, "I saw the bullfight." Both slides were present. The effective global manager sees what is there and works within any business system as it exists.

Perhaps Alvin Toffler set the stage when he wrote, "The transnational corporation . . . may do research in one country, manufacture components in another, assemble them in a third, sell the manufactured goods in a fourth, deposit its surplus funds in a fifth, and so on" [1]. It is a changing, interdependent, pluralistic world, and there are some excellent international managers and organizations dealing with it.

Trivial Pursuit

We would like to invite readers to play the game. Trivial Pursuit is a board game that has sold millions of copies throughout the world. The game requires players to answer questions in a number of categories such as geography, entertainment, history, art and literature, science and nature, and sports. The category of the question is determined by a roll of the dice.

You have rolled the dice and drawn the category "NAFTA." This is your question. "Which country, Canada, the United States, or Mexico, has produced the most competent global people?"

If this question were in Trivial Pursuit, it would be a very difficult question. One word contributes to the difficulty—competent. A standard dictionary provides this definition for competent: "well-qualified, capable, fit."

To get a range of answers, on a recent business trip, we took a informal poll. Here are our results. Some said the United States produced the most competent global people in business. The United States is the biggest economic entity in the history of the world, with dominant positions worldwide in computers, space, medicine, and biology. Its competent global people in business make this possible.

This was overheard by a Mexican who said that Americans are naive globally. American business people, according to him, are the most ethnocentric of all business people. The dictionary describes ethnocentric as "one who judges others by using one's own personal or cultural standards."

Besides, the Mexican said, American business people have their priorities messed up. They are too materialistic, too work-oriented, too time-motivated, and equate anything "new" with best. Americans also have the highest attrition rate (returning early from an international assignment) of any country.

Canadians received some votes, as did Mexicans. But there was no consensus. Since no agreement could be reached on the correct answer to my first question we decided to rephrase it. "What contribution to a global organization is made by managers of various cultures?"

Hari Bedi, an Indian working in Hong Kong, believes that Asian internationals use the five C's: *continuity* (a sense of history and tradition; *commitment* (to the growth of the organization); *connections* (where social skills and social standing count); *compassion* (balancing scientific and political issues); and *cultural sensitivity* (a respect for others' ways).

These qualities are among the contributions made by Asian managers to a multinational organization. According to Bedi, Western managers use the five E's: *expertise* (experience in managerial and technical theory); *ethos* (practical experience); *eagerness* (the enthusiasm of the entrepreneur); *esprit de corps* (a common identity); and *endorsement* (seeks unusual opportunities).

The answer is that the managers of every country contribute something to a multinational organization. The usefulness of that contribution depends on the situation. Competent global people are able to recognize the contribution made by persons from Canada, the United States, and Mexico. They also are able to develop solutions to problems faced by persons involved in NAFTA by using these contributions and cultural diversity as a resource rather than a barrier to be overcome.

Women and NAFTA

The issue is not whether a person is male of female; the issue is one of competency. However, there is some evidence that many women are exceptional global people for the following reasons:

1. They tend to approach relationships and negotiations from a win-win strategy that results in success for both sides rather than the sports oriented win-lose approach of many men.
2. Women tend to be more formal, show more respect, and take more care in establishing relationships than men.
3. Women tend to be better listeners and more sympathetic than men, and, therefore, can tune into the needs and expectations of their foreign counterparts.

Of course, not all women are more globally competent than all men. But women, in general, have the qualities that work well overseas. In light of this, it is paradoxical that so few women have risen to international management positions. Perhaps the opportunities provided by NAFTA will change this.

Should the Boss Stay Home?

"If my boss and the president of our company would stay at home and do what they are best at doing, we would have fewer problems."

Senior executives make it to the top for many reasons. Among them is the ability to make quick decisions that more often than not have positive results. These same executives are often rather articulate in conceptualizing issues. As a result, the executive spends more time talking than listening. The skill of articulation carried to the extreme can become a liability because there is little or no listening.

We learn to listen and talk before we read and write. Listening is a complex activity. The average person speaks approximately 12,000 sentences every day. The average person can speak at about 150 words per minute, while the listener's brain can absorb around 400 words per minute. What do we do with this spare capacity? Unfortunately, many do nothing. We become bored. A good listener is seldom bored and uses this extra capacity to listen to the entire message and to analyze more fully the meanings behind the words. There are various types of listening behaviors.

- *Information gathering* is a form of listening, whose purpose is the absorption of stated facts. Information gathering does not pertain to the interpretation of the facts.
- *Cynical listening* is based on the assumption that all communication is designed to take advantage of the listener. It also is referred to as defensive listening.
- *Offensive listening* is the attempt to trap or trip up an opponent with one's own words. A lawyer, when questioning a witness, listens for contradictions, irrelevancies, and weakness.
- *Polite listening* is listening just enough to meet the minimum social requirements. Many people are not listening—they are just waiting their turn to speak and are perhaps rehearsing their lines. They are not really talking *to* each other, but *at* each other.
- *Active listening* involves a listener with very definite responsibilities. In active listening, the listener strives for complete

and accurate understanding, for empathy, and to actively assist in working out problems.

Providing Feedback

Listening fulfills a vital function. The listener provides feedback to the speaker concerning the other's success in transmitting a message clearly. In doing this, the listener exerts some influence over future messages that might or might not be sent.

The ability to listen is especially important when persons from low-context cultures communicate with persons from high-context cultures. The communication context of Americans and Canadians is low, while Mexicans have a high-context communication. Being aware of these differences can make one a more effective, active listener and better all around communicator. If the boss isn't a good listener, help him or her find reasons to stay home.

Handling Two Swords at the Same Time

To be skillful, effective, and successful in one's own culture by being assertive, quick, and to the point is one mode of behavior. To be equally successful in another culture by being unassertive, patient, and somewhat indirect is another mode entirely—like handling two swords at the same time internationally. Yo Miyoshi, president of H.B. Fuller Japan Co. in Tokyo, says he modifies his behavior to suit his audience. "When I discuss something with the head office in the United States, I try to be Western. But when I deal with people in the company here, I am Oriental or Japanese."

Miyoshi is able to shift his style, or to handle two swords at the same time. He had to learn this behavior. When I confronted executives in my seminars with this necessity, we very quickly began commiserating about this difficulty.

The words listed below are some of the adjectives that could be used to describe an international manager. We ask that persons who are involved in NAFTA review the list and circle the ones that apply:

assertive, energetic, decisive, ambitious, confident, aggressive, quick, competitive, impatient, impulsive, quick-tempered, intelligent, excitable, informal, versatile, persuasive, imaginative, original, witty, colorful, calm, easy-going, good-natured, tactful, unemotional, good listener, inhibited, shy, absent-minded, cautious, methodical, timid, lazy, procrastinator, likes responsibility, resourceful, individualist, broad interests, limited interests, good team worker, likes to work alone, sociable, cooperative, quiet, easily distracted, serious, idealistic, ethnocentric, cynical, conscientious, flexible, mature, dependable, honest, sincere, reliable, loyal, adaptable, curious.

Using these qualities skillfully is handling one sword—the sword that makes one successful in one's business culture. John Ramsey, an American executive of a large public accounting company, expressed it this way: "The reason I'm successful is because I'm assertive, energetic, aggressive, competitive, and an idealist."

The next step in the exercise is to think as an American of your next trip to Canada or Mexico and consider the people you will be meeting. Now, go back to the same list of words and place a check beside those qualities that you believe these people will look for in you. There are a number of differences. The same exercise can be done by Canadians and Mexicans.

We all carry our basic personality characteristics—the sword that made us successful, our aggressiveness and competitiveness, for example. But in another culture the second sword we are expected to carry might be characterized by qualities such as gentleness, cooperativeness, followership, indirectness, and commitment to relationships. Skillful global people involved in NAFTA need to carry two swords.

Making Speeches to Multicultural Audiences

The speaker begins the speech with a joke. It falls flat, so he tells another story. Undaunted by his failure to get any reaction from the audience, he plunges into his talk. It is little more than an unstructured compilation of company case studies linked by flimsy themes. He breezes through the points made, relying on anecdotal evidence to illustrate their practical application.

In the end, one senses the sigh of relief go through the audience when the speaker sits down to polite applause. "It didn't go down particularly well with this audience," was the courteous feedback the speaker was given by organizers. Why?

To begin with, the speaker was an American, who gives most speeches in the United States. The major difference between this speech and others that have been given is the audience. This audience is multicultural. The speaker's initial mistake was to assume that addressing a multicultural audience is no different from speaking to a group of his own culture. Such an assumption can be fatal, especially for persons from Canada, the United States, or Mexico who are called upon to give speeches or make presentations in another country.

Any effective speaker, as a matter of course, must learn to adapt his talks to the expectations of the audience. But when the business audience includes people from different cultures, the challenge is greater. Here are some suggestions on how to avoid some pitfalls.

While speakers in the United States customarily open with a joke, this practice is not usual in Canada or Mexico. Be careful not to identify particular groups, as the other participants will feel left out. Anecdotes that involve drinking are appreciated by Japanese listeners, but not in formal presentations.

The use of gestures, facial expressions, and lively body movements are characteristic of effective speakers in Mexico. However, the excessive use of aggressive, hard-sell techniques can turn off listeners and result in a loss of respect. Canadian audiences are best won over by gentle persuasion.

Empathy

Ideally, as Canadians, Americans, and Mexicans work together in the context of NAFTA, they become more global in perspective and less ethnocentric. When this is coupled with a formal study of the counterpart's language and culture, new insights into ways of improving our interactions and becoming aware of the influence of our culture on our behavior are gained. We then have the possibility of understanding that our culture itself can create obstacles in cross-cultural interactions. These obstacles are compounded when ethnocentrism is in the extreme.

Ethnocentrism also exists in organizations. It might be seen, for example, in those who place only home country personnel in important positions in their worldwide operations. These people are paid more, in the belief that they are more competent, intelligent, and reliable. Lack of ethnocentrism is seen in organizations when superiority and competence are not equated with nationality.

The attitude of non-ethnocentrism in people is probably related to the complex psychosocial development of a tolerant and strong personality. Such personalities are capable of multidimensional thinking, are comfortable with ambiguity, and have high self-esteem.

Non-ethnocentric organizations have similar characteristics. In the village of Supai in northern Arizona, where about 300 Indians lived in peace for several hundred years, there is a sign over the counter in the cafe that reads: "Do not judge another man until you have walked one mile in his moccasins." This is a description of empathy.

In the research of criteria relevant to overseas experience, empathy has been found in all studies to be an important quality for both adjustments and success. Ethnocentrism and empathy are opposites. If one believes in the superiority of one's group and culture and has feelings of contempt toward others, it is impossible to walk in their shoes.

The ability to express empathy varies. Some people show an interest in others clearly—some are unable to project even a superficial interest.

Here are two good measures to determine one's empathy. First, can you work well with people whose values and way of doing things are different from yours? Second, when working with people from different cultures, do you believe and behave in such a way that you are concerned only with end results and not people's feelings or reactions?

A Final Checklist

In a new book, *The Global Challenge: Building the New World Enterprise* [2], the authors identify a number of competencies required to make globalization work. The following are the competencies they believe are most relevant to *NAFTA: Managing Cultural Differences*. After the description of each competency, the reader can assess whether this competency is possessed to a high degree, somewhat, or to a low degree both by the reader and by the key staff involved in NAFTA.

Competency One: Possesses a Global Mindset

A global mindset is an attitude, seeing the cultural complexity of one's environment where occurrences and actions can have a myriad of causes. One must develop the skill to work effectively with different mindsets and customs, discovering "why" people are the way they are.

Competency Two: Able to Work as Collaborators/Equals with Persons from Diverse Backgrounds and Especially Able to Work Effectively with Women

The diversity in most countries has increased recently and this is reflected in a heterogenous work force in most societies. The number of women in the work force at all levels has increased dramatically, as well. Learning to work effectively and sensitively with persons from diverse cultural backgrounds is essential in the globalization process.

Competency Three: Has a Long-Term Orientation

Because a great number of organizations have been tied to the bottom line, year-end profits, and bonuses based on 12-month earnings, 'short-termism' has compromised our ability to compete. Long-term planning, investment, and research will empower global leaders to shift their organization's focus to survive in the mercurial global economy.

Competency Four: Negotiates and Approaches Conflicts in a Collaborative Mode

Most negotiations are difficult and frustrating. Conflict is present in all organizations and can produce a positive outcome if effectively managed. Managing disagreements between negotiators from different cultures requires a synergistic collaboration and often a creative approach for resolution.

Competency Five: Manages Skillfully the Foreign Deployment Cycle

In the past, there was no preparation for an overseas assignment other than, "Are you technically competent and willing to go?" Today a successful overseas assignment includes active recruitment for the assignment, education and training prior to departure, on-going support during the assignment, debriefing, education on re-entry, and thoughtful re-integration back into the corporate culture.

Competency Six: Leads and Participates Effectively in Multicultural Teams

Well-functioning teams can increase productivity and creativity. However, functioning skillfully on a team is a learned skill. Generally, the more groups have in common, the easier it is to form teams. In today's work place, most teams will be characterized by persons from culturally diverse backgrounds. The productivity of culturally diverse teams has great potential, as does the complexity of leading and managing these heterogeneous groups.

Competency Seven: Understands One's Culture, Values, and Assumptions

A global manager must have a high degree of cultural self-awareness to accept and understand the relativity of culture. There is no absolutely correct way of doing anything. A person will effectively communicate and work with others from different cultures when their own culture is deeply understood.

Competency Eight: Accurately Profiles Organizational Culture and National Culture of Others

Every society has a set of beliefs, assumptions and values that hold that culture together and make it cohesive. Behavior is not random, it is highly predictable most of the time.

Competency Nine: Avoids Cultural Mistakes and Behaves in a Manner that Demonstrates Knowledge of and Respect for the Way of Conducting Business in Other Countries

Skillful global managers know there is no single way of effectively conducting business that works all over the world. Learning the customs and courtesies of one's global partners is the norm rather than the exception.

References

1. Toffler, A. *The Third Wave*. New York: Morrow, 1980.
2. Moran, R. and Riesenberger J. *The Global Challenge: Building the New World Enterprise*. London: Mc-Graw-Hill, 1994.

Resources for Additional Information

Mexico

Finding sources of information in Mexico requires patience and perseverance. The data available is decidedly regional in almost every aspect. Contacting the same organization or source in different cities may produce different answers and results. The infrastructure for data gathering and analysis, especially financial data, is in its infancy in Mexico. Many sources have been inundated with requests for data since NAFTA was implemented. Expect to wait for a response.

The sources listed are categorized by the three major business centers in Mexico: Mexico, Monterrey, and Guadalajara. When contacting these organizations, understand that a personal visit will produce much better results than a fax or phone call. Also realize that routine data common in the U.S., such as sector analysis, is generally non-existent in Mexico. Finally, imprecise requests will probably receive no response at all. Some of the best material available in Mexico is in publication form from the American Chamber of Commerce, such as *A Guide to Mexico for Business, American Companies Operating in Mexico,* and *How to Sell Your Product in Mexico.*

A list of sources follows [1].

---

[1] Prepared by John K. Barrett, Executive Director of The American Chamber of Commerce of Mexico, A.C. in Monterrey, Mexico. The sources of information provided were accurate as of 1 February 1994. The comments at the beginning of this section are not necessarily reflective of the American Chamber of Commerce, Mexico.

Mexico City

United States Embassy
Reforma 305
Col Cuahuatemos
06500 Mexico, D.F.
Tel: (525) 211-0042,
207-5307

American Chamber of
Commerce
Lucerna 78
Col. Juarez
06600 Mexico, D.F.
Tel: (525) 724-3800
Fax: (525) 701-3908

Secretaria de Relaciones
Exteriores
Asuntos Economicos
R. Flores Magon No. 1,
14 Floor
Tlatelolco, Mexico, D.F.
Tel: (525) 782-3312, 202-7804

Camara Nacional de
Comercio (CANACO)
Reforma 42
Col. Centro
06048 Mexico, D.F.
Tel: (525) 593-5847, 546-0005
Fax: (525) 664-3039

Canadian Embassy
Schiller 529
Col. Polanco, De. M. Hidalgo
11560 Mexico, D.F.

Tel: (525) 724-7900
Fax: (525) 724-7982

Secretaia de Comercio y
Fomento Industrial (SECOFI)
Calle Alfonso Reyes No. 30
Col. Condesa
06140 Mexico, D.F.
Tel: (525) 211-3545
Fax: (525) 224-3000

Secretaria de Hacienda y
Credito Publico
Avenida Hidalgo 77,
Modulo 1
Planta Baja, Col. Guerrero
Del Cuauhtemoe

BANCOMEXT
Centro de Servicios al
Comercio Exterior
Periferico Sur 3025,
3rd Floor
Heroes de Padierna
10700 Mexico
Tel: (525) 683-7055

NAFINSA
Offica of Foreign Investment
Promotion
Insurgentes Sur 1971
Torre 3, Piso 13
Col. Guadalupe Inn
01020 Mexico, D.F.
Tel: (525) 325-6674, 325-6619

Monterrey

American Consulate General
Commercial Attache
Ave. Constitucion, 411 Pte.
64000 Monterrey, N.L.
Tel: (528) 345-2120, 340-9705
Fax: (528) 342-0177

Canadian Consulate
Zaragoza 1300 Sur, Desp. 108
Edificio Kalos
64000 Monterrey, N.L.
Tel: (528) 344-3200
Fax: (528) 3048

American Chamber of Commerce
Pichachos 760, Desp. 4
Col Obispado
64060 Monterrey, N.L.
Tel: (528) 348-0414, 348-7141
Fax: (528) 358-5574

ProExport Nuevo Leon
Ave. Consitucion 419 Pte.
Edificio Hinsa 5 Piso
64000 Monterrey, N.L.
Tel: (528) 345-7354, 345-7355
Fax: (528) 344-5576

Secretaria de Desarrollo
Economico
Zaragoza 1300 Sur, 4 Piso
Edificio Kalos
64000 Monterrey, N.L.
Tel: (528) 345-3032, 345-0031
Fax: (528) 345-1062

SECOFI
Fundidora 501, 1 Piso
Col Obrera
64010 Monterrey, N.L.
Tel: (528) 369-6481 to 86
Fax: (528) 369-6487

Secretaria de Programacion y
Desarrollo de Coahuila
Victoria 406 Pte. 3 Piso
25000 Saltillo, Coah.
Tel: (528) 412-3903, 412-8723
Fax: (528) 412-4320

Banco Nacional de Comercio
Exterior del Noreste
Ave. Lazaro Cardenas 2499 Pte.
66260 Garza Garcia, N.L.
Tel: (528) 363-0300, 363-0090
Fax: (528) 363-0858

Camara de la Industria de la
Transformacion de Nuevo Leon
Ocampo 250 Pte. 4 Piso
Edificio de las Instituciones
64000 Monterrey, N.L.
Tel: (528) 345-6215, 345-5440
Fax: (528) 344-0227

Camara Nacional de Comercio
Ocampo 250 Pte. 1 Piso
Edificio de las Instituciones
64000 Monterrey, N.L.
Tel: (528) 342-2169, 344-5255
Fax: (528) 345-6700

Consejo Nacional de
Comercio Exterior del Noreste
Ocampo 250 Pte. 7 Piso
Edificio de las Instituciones
64000 Monterrey, N.L.
Tel: (528) 342-2143, 342-2144
Fax: (528) 342-8207

Secretaria de Relaciones
Exteriores
Loma Redonda 2702
Col. Lomas de San Francisco
64710 Monterrey, N.L.
Tel: (528) 347-4191, 347-3319
Fax: (528) 347-3361

Guadalajara

American Consulate General
Progreso 175
44160 Guadalajara, Jal.
Tel: (523) 625-2700, 625-2998

American Chamber of
Commerce
Av. Moctezuma No. 442
Col Jardines del Sol
45050 Zapopan, Jal.
Tel: (523) 634-6606
Fax: (523) 634-7374

SECOFI
Av. Mariano Otero 3431
1 Y 2 Piso
Col. Valle Verde
44550 Guadalajara, Jal.
Tel: (523) 621-0694, 621-1642

Banco National de Comercio
Exterior
Miguel Blanco 883
Sector Juarez
44100 guadalajara, Jal.
Tel: (523) 658-0980, 658-1108
Fax: (523) 658-2388

National Assoc. of Imports
and Exports
Av. de la Paz No. 2530
Sector Juarez
44100 Guadalajara, Jal.
Tel: (523) 615-0177, 630-1206
Fax: (523) 615-2796

Camara Regional de la Industria
Av. Washington No. 1920
3 y 4 Pisos
Col. Moderna, Sector Juarez
44100 Guadalajara, Jal.
Tel: (523) 611-3039, 611-3276
Fax: (523) 611-1207

Camra Nacional de Comercio
Av. Vallarta No. 4095
44100 Guadalajara, Jal.
Tel: (523) 647-1026, 647-3052

Secretaria de Promocion y
Desarrollo Economico del
Estado
Prolg. Av. Alcalde 1351
44100 Guadalajara, Jal.
Tel: (523) 623-3972, 653-1994

Canadian Consulate
Hotel Fiesta Americana
Tel: (523) 616-5642, Ext. 3005

Canada

Business people looking for information in or about Canada can take advantage of the fact that Canada has one of the most sophisticated systems for gathering and disseminating information in the world. For example, Statistics Canada, the federal statistical agency, is an internationally recognized leader in the preparation of data on economic, demographic, and social issues. Moreover, the Canadian government recognizes that it has a vital role to play in providing information to business, especially in areas such as investment, economic development, market intelligence, regulation, taxation, customs and tariffs, government programs and services, sources of assistance, referrals, and contacts.

In looking for information in Canada, the business person will be aided by the fact that Canadians do a lot of business over the phone. In addition, facsimile machines are found in virtually every office and institution, allowing for instantaneous transmission of hard copy. Moreover, new forms for delivering information are continuously being explored so business users may receive information in a variety of media.

The Canadian federal government, business associations, non-government institutions, and the private sector tend to work closely together. Not only is there an emphasis on partnering within Canada, but there is a recognition that Canadians, in general, must seek partnerships abroad. Several computer-based systems have been created to help foreign businesses find appropriate Canadian partners. For example, the Department of Foreign Affairs and International Trade manages the World Information Network for Exports (WIN Exports), providing users with information about the capabilities, experience, and interests of more that 30,000 Canadian exporters. The Business Opportunities Sourcing System (BOSS) is a database operated by Industry Canada containing profiles of more than 26,000 potential Canadian suppliers. The Business Cooperation Network (BCNet), managed by the Canadian Chamber of Commerce is a computerized match-making system designed to facilitate contacts between Canadian and foreign firms looking for international partnerships.

Foreign business people looking to do business in Canada should start by consulting the appropriate departments of the federal government. Among the best places to begin are the Department of Foreign Affairs and International Trade, Industry Canada, and Revenue Canada (Customs and Excise). Business people looking to invest in Canada should contact Investment Canada, a division of the Department of Foreign Affairs. More specialized interest can be pursued through Agriculture Canada (processed foods) or the Department of Natural Resources (energy, mining forestry). Under the terms of NAFTA, all businesses based in North America are eligible for consideration in larger procurement contracts issued by the Canadian government. Information about procurement opportunities can be obtained from the Department of Supply and Services.

A list of sources follows [2].

Canadian Government Departments and Services in Canada

Department of Foreign Affairs and International Trade (Ottawa)

Department of Foreign Affairs and International Trade (DFAIT) is the Canadian federal government department most directly responsible for trade development. The InfoEx Centre is the first contact point for advice on how to start exporting; it provides information on export-related programs and services; helps find fast answers to export problems; acts as the entry point to DFAIT's trade information network; and can provide interested companies with copies of specialized export publications.

InfoEx Centre
Tel: 1-800-267-8376 or (613) 994-4000
Fax: (613) 996-9709

---

[2] The following list of sources and contacts was provided by Prospectus Inc., an Ottawa-based Canadian firm specializing in the production of practical handbooks and planning tools for business.

Latin America and Caribbean Trade Division
Latin America and Caribbean Trade Division promotes trade with Mexico. There are several trade commissioners at the Embassy of Canada in Mexico City, and there is a satellite office in Monterrey. Trade Commissioners can provide a range of services, including introducing Canadian companies to potential customers in Mexico, advising on marketing channels, assisting those wishing to participate in trade fairs, helping identify suitable Mexican firms to act as agents, and compiling credit and business information on potential foreign customers.

Latin America and Caribbean Trade Division (LGT)
Department of Foreign Affairs and International Trade
Lester B. Pearson Building
125 Sussex Drive
Ottawa, ON K1A 0G2
Tel: (613) 996-6547
Fax: (613) 943-8806

International Trade Centres
International Trade Centres have been established across the country as a first point of contact to support the exporting efforts of Canadian firms. Co-located with the regional offices of Industry Canada (IC), the centres operate under the guidance of DFAIT and all have resident Trade Commissioners. They help companies determine whether or not they are ready to export; assist firms with marketing research and market planning; provide access to government programs designed to promote exports; and arrange for assistance from the Trade Development Division in Ottawa and trade officers abroad. Contact the International Trade Centre nearest you:

British Columbia

Scotia Tower
900-650 West Georgia Street
P.O. Box 11610
Vancouver, BC V6B 5H8
Tel: (604) 666-0434
Fax: (604) 666-8330

Yukon

300 Main Street
Room 210
Whitehorse, YT Y1A 2B5
Tel: (403) 667-3925
Fax: (403) 668-5003

Alberta and Northwest Territories

Canada Place
Suite 540
9700 Jasper Avenue
Edmonton, AB T5J 4C3
Tel: (403) 495-2944
Fax: (403) 495-4507

510-5th Street S.W.
11th Floor
Calgary, AB T5P 3S2
Tel: (403) 292-6660
Fax: (403) 292-4578

Saskatchewan

119-4th Avenue South
Suite 401
Saskatoon, SK S7K 5X2
Tel: (306) 975-5315
Fax: (306) 975-5334

1919 Saskatchewan Drive
6th Floor
Regina, SK S4P 3V7
Tel: (306) 780-6325
Fax: (306) 780-6679

Manitoba

330 Portage Avenue
7th Floor
P.O. Box 981
Winnipeg, MB R3C 2V2
Tel: (204) 983-8036
Fax: (204) 983-2187

Ontario

Dominion Public Building
4th Floor
1 Front Street West
Toronto, ON M5J 1A4
Tel: (416) 973-5053
Fax: (416) 973-8161

Quebec

Stock Exchange Tower
800 Victoria Square
Suite 3800
P.O. Box 247
Montreal, PQ H4Z 1E8
Tel: (514) 283-8185
Fax: (514) 283-8794

New Brunswick

Assumption Place
770 Main Street
P.O. Box 1210
Moncton, NB E1C 8P9
Tel: (506) 851-6452
Fax: (506) 851-6429

Prince Edward Island

Confederation Court Mall
134 Kent Street
Suite 400
P.O. Box 1115
Charlottetown, PE C1A 7M8
Tel: (902) 566-7400
Fax: (902) 566-7450

Nova Scotia

Central Guaranty Trust Tower
1801 Hollis Street
5th Floor
P.O. Box 940, Stn M
Halifax, NS B3J 2V9
Tel: (902) 426-7540
Fax: (902) 426-2624

Newfoundland

Atlantic Place
215 Water Street
Suite 504
P.O. Box 8950
St. John's, NF A1B 3R9
Tel: (709) 772-5511
Fax: (709) 772-5093/2373

World Information Network for Exports

The World Information Network for Exports (WIN Exports) is
a computer-based information system designed by DFAIT to
help Canada's trade development officers abroad match foreign
needs to Canadian capabilities. It provides users with information on the capabilities, experience, and interests of more than
30,000 Canadian exporters. To be registered on WIN Exports,
call: (613) 996-5701.

Program for Export Market Development (PEMD)

This program seeks to increase export sales by sharing the
costs of industry-initiated activities aimed at developing export
markets. PEMD is administered by IC regional offices and funded
by DFAIT. Activities eligible for PEMD financial support (up to
50 percent of the costs) include:

- participation in recognized foreign trade fairs outside of
  Canada
- trips to identify export markets and visits by foreign buyers
  to Canada
- project bidding or proposal preparation at the pre-contractual
  stage for projects outside Canada
- the establishment of permanent sales offices abroad to undertake sustained marketing efforts
- special activities for non-profit, non-sales food, agriculture
  and fish organizations, marketing boards and agencies, trade
  fairs, technical trials, and product demonstrations (for
  example)

- new eligible costs include: product testing for market certification, legal fees for marketing agreements abroad, transportation costs for offsore company trainees, product demonstration costs, and other costs necessary to execute the marketing plan

Support also is provided for certain types of government-planned activities, such as outgoing trade missions of Canadian business representatives and incoming missions to Canada of foreign business and government officials who can influence export sales.

For information, call (613) 954-2858.

International Financing Institutions

DFAIT helps Canadian exporters interested in pursuing multilateral business opportunities financed by international financing institutions (IFI). Canadian exporters and trade associations can access market data, obtain a better understanding of the competition, and determine if an IFI-funded market opportunity is practical and worth pursuing. DFAIT can provide information and advice on the availability of Canadian government-funded assistance programs and can assist companies in developing effective export marketing. For further information contact:

International Finance Division
Department of Foreign Affairs and International Trade
Tel: (613) 995-7251
Fax: (613) 943-1100

Technology Inflow Program

Managed by DFAIT and delivered domestically by the National Research Council, this program is designed to help Canadian companies locate, acquire, and adopt foreign technologies by promoting international collaboration. IC also helps in program promotion. The program officers respond to requests to identify technology sources and opportunities for cooperation between

Canadian and foreign firms. The program will also help Canadian firms make exploratory visits abroad to identify and gain firsthand knowledge of relevant foreign technologies, as well as to negotiate to acquire them.

For information, call (613) 993-3996.

Investment Development Program

This program helps Canadian companies find the investment they need. It actively promotes investments that take the form of new plant and equipment, joint ventures, or strategic partnerships. It is especially interested in attracting investment that introduces new technology into Canada, a key to creating new jobs and economic opportunities. Investment officers make contact with foreign investors and bring them together with Canadian companies. For information, call (613) 996-8625.

Industry Canada

Industry Canada (IC) was created with a broad mandate to improve the competitiveness of Canadian industry. In the area of small business, it has been given specific responsibility to:

- develop, implement and promote national policies to foster the international competitiveness of industry, the enhancement of industrial, scientific and technological development, and the improvement in the productivity and efficiency of industry
- promote the mobility of goods, services, and factors of production within Canada
- develop and implement national policies to foster entrepreneurship and the start-up, growth, and expansion of small businesses
- develop and implement national policies and programs respecting industrial benefits from procurement of goods and services by the government of Canada
- promote and provide support services for the marketing of Canadian goods, services, and technology
- promote investment in Canadian industry, science and technology

IC Regional Offices

The regional offices work directly with Canadian companies to promote industrial, scientific, and technological development. They help clients recognize opportunities in a competitive international marketplace by providing services in the areas of business intelligence and information, technology and industrial development, and trade and market development. They also promote and manage a portfolio of programs and services.

The following are areas in which IC regional offices have special competence:

- access to trade and technology intelligence and expertise
- entry points to national and international networks
- industry sector knowledge base
- co-location with International Trade Centres connected to DFAIT and Canadian posts abroad
- client focus on emerging and threshold firms
- IC Business Intelligence

The Business Opportunities Sourcing System (BOSS)

BOSS is a computerized databank that profiles over 26,000 Canadian companies. It lists basic information on products, services, and operations that is useful to potential customers. The system was established in 1980 by IC in cooperation with participating provincial governments. BOSS was originally established so that Trade Commissioners posted around the world by DFAIT could find Canadian companies that might be able to take advantage of foreign market opportunities. Today, more than 11,000 domestic and international subscribers use the system not only to locate Canadian suppliers but also to obtain market intelligence and identify market opportunities. The majority of subscribers are Canadian companies.

Call (613) 954-5031.

Market Intelligence Service

This service provides Canadian business with detailed market information on a product-specific basis. The service assists

Canadian companies in the exploitation of domestic, export, technology transfer, and new manufacturing investment opportunities. The intelligence is used by Canadian business in decisions regarding manufacturing, product development, marketing, and market expansion. The information includes values, volume and unit price of imports, characteristics of specific imports (e.g., material, grade, price range, etc.), names of importers, major countries of export, identification of foreign exporters to Canada, Canadian production, Canadian exports, and U.S. imports. Two-thirds of the clientele for this service are small businesses.

Call (613) 954-4970.

Revenue Canada
NAFTA Information Desk
Revenue Canada - Customs, Excise and Taxation
6th floor
191 Laurier Avenue West
Ottawa, ON KIA 0L5
Tel: 1-800-661-6121
Fax: (613) 954-4494

NAFTA Spanish Help Desk
Revenue Canada Customs provides a NAFTA Help Desk telephone line with service available in Spanish
Tel: (613) 941-0965

Canadian International Development Agency

An important possible source of financing for Canadian ventures in Mexico is the special fund available through the Canadian International Development Agency (CIDA) under the Industrial Cooperation Program or CIDA/INC. CIDA's Industrial Cooperation Program provides financial contributions to stimulate Canadian private-sector involvement in developing countries by supporting long-term business relationships such as joint ventures and licencing arrangements. INC supports the development of linkages with the private sector in Mexico encouraging Canadian enterprises to share their skills and experiences with partners in Mexico and other countries. A series of INC mechanisms helps enterprises to establish mutually beneficial collaborative arrangements for the transfer of technology and the creation of employment in Mexico.

There are five INC mechanisms which help eligible Canadian firms to conduct studies and provide professional guidance and advice to potential clients. Where a project involves environmental improvement, technology transfer, developmental assistance to women, job training, or job creation, early contact with CIDA's Industrial Cooperation Division is suggested.

An important CIDA criterion is that the project creates jobs in Mexico without threatening jobs in Canada. In fact, most CIDA-assisted projects have produced net increases in Canadian jobs.

Industrial Cooperation Division
Canadian International Development Agency
200, Promenade du Portage
Hull, PQ K1A 0G4
Tel: (819) 997-7905/7906
Fax: (819) 953-5024

Atlantic Canada Opportunities Agency

Atlantic Canadian companies seeking to develop exports to Mexico may be eligible for assistance from the Atlantic Canada Opportunities Agency (ACOA). The Agency works in partnership with entrepreneurs from the Atlantic region to promote self-sustaining economic activity in Atlantic Canada.

The ACOA Action Program provides support to businesses as they look to expand existing markets through the development of marketing plans. Efforts include monitoring trade opportunities arising from global economic change, communications efforts to promote the region, trade missions and associated activities, as well as better coordination with federal and provincial bodies that influence trade and investment opportunities.

ACOA Head Office   Toll free: 1-800-561-7862
Blue Cross Centre   Fax: (506) 851-7403
644 Main Street
P.O. Box 6051   Newfoundland and Labrador
Moncton, NB E1C 9J8   Suite 801, Atlantic Place

215 Water Street
P.O. Box 1060, Station C
St. John's, NF A1C 5M5
Tel: (709) 772-2751
Toll free: 1-800-563-5766
Fax: (709) 772-2712

Nova Scotia
Suite 600
1801 Hollis Street
P.O. Box 2284, Station M
Halifax, NS B3J 3M5
Tel: (902) 426-8361
Toll free: 1-800-565-1228
Fax: (902) 426-2054

Prince Edward Island
75 Fitzroy Street
3rd Floor
Charlottetown, PE C1A 1R6
Tel: (902) 566-7492
Toll free: 1-800-565-0228
Fax: (902) 566-7098

New Brunswick
570 Queen Street
P.O. Box 578
Fredericton, NB E3B 5A6
Tel: (506) 452-3184
Toll free: 1-800-561-4030
Fax: (506) 452-3285

Western Economic Diversification Canada

Western Canadian companies interested in Mexico may be able to secure assistance from Western Economic Diversification Canada (WD). This agency provides financial assistance for projects that contribute to the diversification of the western economy. It acts as a pathfinder to ensure that western businesses are aware of and receive assistance from the most appropriate source of funding, federal or other, for their projects. It acts as an advocate for the west in national economic decision-making and it coordinates federal activities that have an impact on economic growth in the west. It also plays a role in promoting trade between western Canada and markets around the world. Inquiries about the Western Diversification Program and other activities of the department can be directed to any of the following regional offices:

Manitoba
P.O. Box 777
Suite 712
The Cargill Building
240 Graham Avenue
Winnipeg, MB R3C 2L4

Tel: (204) 983-4472
Fax: (204) 983-4694

Saskatchewan
P.O. Box 2025
Suite 601

S.J. Cohen Building
119-4th Avenue South
Saskatoon, SK S7K 5X2
Tel: (306) 975-4373
Fax: (306) 975-5484
Toll free within Regina
city limits
Tel: (306) 780-6725

Alberta
Canada Place, Suite 1500
9700 Jasper Avenue
Edmonton, AB T5J 4H7
Tel: (403) 495-4164

Fax: (403) 495-7725
Toll free within Calgary
city limits
Tel: (403) 292-5382

British Columbia
P.O. Box 49276
Bentall Tower 4
1200-1055 Dunsmuir Street
Vancouver, BC V7X 1L3
Tel: (604) 666-6256
Fax: (604) 666-2353
Toll free within the Province
Tel: 1-800-663-2008

Export Development Corporation

EDC is a unique financial institution that helps Canadian business compete internationally. EDC facilitates export trade and foreign investment by providing risk management services, including insurance and financing, to Canadian companies and their global customers.

EDC's programs fall into four major categories:

- export credit insurance, covering short- and medium-sized credits
- performance-related guarantees and insurance, providing coverage for exporters and financial institutions against calls on various performance bonds and obligations normally issued either by banks or surety companies
- foreign investment insurance, providing political risk protection for new Canadian investments abroad
- export financing, providing medium- and long-term export financing to foreign buyers of Canadian goods and services.

For information on the full range of EDC services, contact any of the following EDC offices:

Ottawa (Head Office)
151 O'Connor Street
Ottawa, ON K1A 1K3
Tel: (613) 598-2500
Fax: (613) 237-2690

Public Information
Tel: (613) 598-2739

Vancouver
Suite 1030
One Bentall Centre
505 Burrard Street
Vancouver, BC V7X 1M5
Tel: (604) 666-6234
Fax: (604) 666-7550

Calgary
Suite 1030
510-5th Street S.W.
Calgary, AB T2P 3S2
Tel: (403) 292-6898
Fax: (403) 292-6902

Winnipeg
8th Floor
330 Portage Avenue
Winnipeg, MB R3C 0C4
Tel: (204) 983-5114
Fax: (204) 983-2187
(serving Manitoba and
Saskatchewan)

Toronto
Suite 810
National Bank Building
150 York Street
P.O. Box 810
Toronto, ON M5H 3S5
Tel: (416) 973-6211
Fax: (416) 862-1267

London
Suite 1512
Talbot Centre
148 Fullarton Street
London, ON N6A 5P3
Tel: (519) 645-5828
Fax: (519) 645-5580

Montreal
Suite 4520
800 Victoria Square
P.O. Box 124
Tour de la Bourse
Montreal, PQ H4Z 1C3
Tel: (514) 283-3013
Fax: (514) 878-9891

Halifax
Purdy's Wharf, Tower 2
Suite 1410
1969 Upper Water Street
Halifax, NS B3J 3R7
Tel: (902) 429-0426
Fax: (902) 423-0881

National Research Council

Canadian companies hoping to succeed in the Mexican marketplace may require additional technology to improve their competitiveness. The National Research Council (NRC) works with Canadian firms of all sizes to develop and apply technology for economic benefit. The Council supervises the Industrial Research Assistance Program (IRAP), a national network for the diffusion and transfer of technology.

The IRAP network supports the process of developing, accessing, acquiring, implanting, and using technology throughout Canadian industry. IRAP has been in existence for 40 years and has acquired a reputation as one of the more flexible and effective federal programs. IRAP takes advantage of an extensive network that includes more than 120 regional and local offices, 20 provincial technology centres, the Council's own laboratories and research institutes, federal government departments, and technology transfer offices in Canadian universities. The IRAP network also extends abroad through the technology counsellors attached to Canadian posts in some 18 foreign countries. For more information or the name of the IRAP office nearest you, contact the following:

IRAP Office
National Research Council
Montreal Road
Building M-55
Ottawa, ON K1A 0R6
Tel: (613) 993-5326
Fax: (613) 952-1086

Key Contacts in Canada

Professional Associations
Canadian Construction
Association (CCA)
85 Albert Street
Ottawa, Canada K1P 6A4
Tel: (613) 236-9455
Fax: (613) 239-9526

Association of Consulting
Engineers of Canada (ACEC)
Suite 616, 130 Albert St
Ottawa, Canada K1P 5G4
Tel: (613) 236-0569
Fax: (613) 236-6193

Royal Architectural Institute
of Canada (RAIC)
Suite 330, 55 Murray Street
Ottawa, Canada K1N 5M3
Tel: (613) 232-7165
Fax: (613) 232-7559

Business Associations

The Canadian Council for the Americas (CCA) is a non-profit organization formed in 1987 to promote business interests in Latin American and Caribbean countries. The CCA promotes events and programs targeted at expanding business and building networking contacts between Canada and the countries of the region. It also publishes a bimonthly newsletter.

The Canadian Council for the
Americas (CCA)
Executive Offices, 3rd Floor
145 Richmond Street West
Toronto, ON M5H 2L2
Tel: (416) 367-4313
Fax: (416) 367-5460

The Canadian Chamber of
Commerce (CCC)
55 Metcalfe Street,
Suite 1160
Ottawa, ON K1P 6N4
Tel: (613) 238-4000
Fax: (613) 238-7643

Canadian Exporters'
Association (CEA)
99 Bank Street, Suite 250
Ottawa, ON K1P 6B9
Tel: (613) 238-8888
Fax: (613) 563-9218

Forum for International Trade
and Training (FITT)
155 Queen Street,
Suite 608
Ottawa, ON K1P 6L1
Tel: (613) 230-3553
Fax: (613) 230-6808

Canadian Manufacturers'
Association (CMA)
75 International Boulevard,
4th Floor
Etobicoke, ON M9W 6L9
Tel: (416) 798-8000
Fax: (416) 798-8050

Language Information Centre
240 Sparks Street, RPO
Box 55011
Ottawa, ON K1P 1A1
Tel: (613) 523-3510

Canadian Freight Forwarders
Association (CIFFA)
Box 929
Streetsville, ON L5M 2C5
Tel: (905) 567-4633
Fax: (905) 542-2716

Bank of Montreal, International Offices in Canada
The Bank of Montreal is the longest-serving Canadian bank in Mexico. It offers a wide range of international banking services and trade financing through its Trade Finance offices across Canada.

Trade Finance Offices:
129 St. James Street West,
12th Floor
Montreal, PQ H2Y 1L6
Tel: (514) 877-9465
Fax: (514) 877-6933

First Canadian Place
23rd Floor
Toronto, ON M5X 1A1
Tel: (416) 867-5584
Fax: (416) 867-7635

959 Burrard Street, 6th Floor
P.O. Box 49350
Vancouver, BC V7X 1L5
Tel: (604) 665-2740
Fax: (604) 665-7283

International Operations
Offices:
959 Burrard Street, 7th floor
P.O. Box 49500
Vancouver, BC V7X 1L5

Tel: (604) 665-3705
Fax: (604) 665-7120

B1 Level, FCC, 340-7th
Avenue South West
Calgary, AB T2P 0X4
Tel: (403) 234-3775
Fax: (403) 234-3777

335 Main Street, P.O. Box 844
Winnipeg, MB R3C 2R6
Tel: (204) 985-2202
Fax: (204) 985-2739

234 Simcoe Street, 3rd Floor
Toronto, ON M5T 1T1
Tel: (416) 867-6567
Fax: (416) 867-7162

288 St. James St. West
Montreal, PQ H2Y 1N1
Tel: (514) 877-7317
Fax: (514) 877-7155

Baker & McKenzie Offices
Baker & McKenzie is one of the largest international law firms with offices in 35 countries. They presently have four offices in Mexico, in the cities of Juárez, Mexico City, Monterrey, and Tijuana. In addition to providing legal advice, the firm's offices in Canada and Mexico work to assist Canadian companies to find the right partner to enable them to establish or expand their activities in Mexico.

Baker & McKenzie
Barristers & Solicitors
112 Adelaide Street East
Toronto, ON M5C 1K9
Tel: (416) 865-6910/6903
Fax: (416) 863-6275

Mexican Government Offices

The Embassy of Mexico, Mexican Trade Commissioners in Canada, and Mexican consulates can provide assistance and guidance to Canadian companies in need of information about doing business in Mexico.

Embassy of Mexico
130 Albert Street, Suite 1800
Ottawa, ON K1P 5G4
Tel: (613) 233-8988
Fax: (613) 235-9123

Mexican Consulate in
Ottawa
Tel: (613) 235-7782

SECOFI
130 Albert Street, Suite 1700
Ottawa, ON K1P 5G4
Tel: (613) 235-7782
Fax: (613) 235-1129

Other Mexican Consulates
General in Canada

Consulate General of Mexico
2000 Mansfield Street,
Suite 1015
Montreal, PQ H3A 2Z7
Tel: (514) 288-2502/4916
Fax: (514) 288-8287

Consulate General of Mexico
60 Bloor Street West, Suite 203
Toronto, ON M4W 3B8
Tel: (416) 922-2718/3196
Fax: (416) 922-8867

Consulate General of Mexico
810-1139 West Pender Street
Vancouver, BC V6E 4A4
Tel: (604) 684-3547/1859
Fax: (604) 684-2485

Mexican Honorary Consulate
380, Chemin St. Louis
No. 1407

Québec, PQ G1S 4M1
Tel: (418) 681-3192
Fax: (418) 683-7843

Mexican Honorary Consulate
830-540 5th Avenue, S.W.
Calgary, AB T2P 0M2
Tel: (403) 263-7077/7078
Fax: (403) 263-7075

For the Mexican Trade Commission offices in Montreal, Toronto, and Vancouver see the following listing for Bancomext.

Mexican Banks with Offices in Canada

Bancomext offers credits, export guarantees, and counselling services for those seeking to do business in Mexico. Credits are available for export, import, and project financing. Counselling covers fiscal, financial, marketing, and legal aspects of commercial transactions. Bancomext also sponsors trade fairs, international exhibitions, and trade missions.

Bancomext
Trade Commission of Mexico
P.O. Box 32, Suite 2712
TD Bank Tower
66 Wellington Street
Toronto, ON M5K 1A1
Tel: (416) 867-9292
Fax: (416) 867-1847

Bancomext
Trade Commission of Mexico
200 Granville Street,

Suite 1365
Vancouver, BC V6C 1S4
Tel: (604) 682-3648
Fax: (604) 682-1355

Bancomext
Trade Commission of Mexico
1501 McGill College,
Suite 1540
Montreal, PQ H3A 3M8
Tel: (514) 287-1669
Fax: (514) 287-1844

Banamex and Banca Serfin are private sector banks that offer specialized services through their international trade information centres. The centres participate in a computerized communications network with access to numerous economic, governmental, and financial data bases throughout the world. These banks are located throughout Mexico, and maintain offices in Toronto.

Banamex	Banca Serfin
(Banco Nacional de México)	161 Bay Street
Suite 3430	BCE Place
1 First Canadian Place	Canada Trust Tower
P.O. Box 299	Suite 4360
Toronto, ON M5X 1C9	P.O. Box 606
Tel: (416) 368-1399	Toronto, ON M5J 2S1
Fax: (416) 367-2543	Tel: (416) 360-8900
	Fax: (416) 360-1760

United States

Selected U.S. Government Resources:

NAFTA Facts: 24 Hour Automated Information System providing information on NAFTA Implementation, Tariff Rates, Rules of Origin, and Doing Business in Canada and Mexico.

Tel: (202) 482-4464, and order menu. After you obtain menu, use that telephone number to choose item on menu and the material will be faxed to you within 12 hours. NAFTA Facts: Canada (202) 482-3101

National Trade Data Bank: CD-Rom database updated monthly. Subscription fee. Tel: (202) 482-1986

Trade Information Center of the U.S. Government provides general information to companies interested in exporting to Mexico and Canada. Advises companies on services available from the government and on documentation necessary to export to Mexico and Canada. Tel: 1-800-USA-TRADE.

- Anti-dumping and countervailing duty matters
  Status of investigations
  Office of Investigations

Import Administration, U.S.
Department of Commerce (DOC),
(202) 482-5403; fax (202) 482-1059
Status of cases
  Office of Antidumping Compliance
  Import Administration, DOC
  (202) 482-2104; fax (202) 482-5105

  Office of Countervailing Compliance
  Import Administration, DOC
  (202) 482-2786; fax (202) 482-4001
subject to NAFTA Dispute Settlement Proceedings
• NAFTA Secretariat, DOC (202) 482-5438;
  fax (202) 482-0148
Agriculture
  NAFTA provisions
  Mexico Desk
  U.S. Dept. of Agriculture
  (202) 720-1340; fax (202) 690-2079

  Canadian Desk
  U.S. Dept. of Agriculture
  (202) 720-1336; fax (202) 690-2079

  Export Services of U.S. Dept of Agriculture
  (202) 720-6343; fax (202) 720-4374

  U.S. Embassy in Mexico City
  Agricultural Trade Office
  011-525-202-0168
Automotive trade
  Mexican automotive policy issues and NAFTA
  Office of Mexico, DOC
  (202) 482-0300; fax (202) 482-5865

  Auto parts and Mexican automotive commercial
  issues
  Parts Division
  Offices of Automotive Affairs, DOC
  (202) 482-5784; fax (202) 482-0674

  NAFTA Automotive Standards Council
  National Highway Traffic Safety Administration

Dept. of Transportation
(202) 366-2114; fax (202) 366-2106
Business travellers
To obtain visa, contact Mexican consular office. Obtain
list of such offices through NAFTA Facts
(202) 482-4464 or
Canadian Consular Offices through NAFTA Facts:
Canada (202) 482-3101
General information
Office of Mexican Affairs
Dept. of State
(202) 647-9292; fax (202) 647-5752
Office of Canadian Affairs
Dept. of State
(202) 647-2170; fax (202) 647-4088
Customs
NAFTA Facts
(202) 482-4464
DOC Trade Information Center 1-800-USA-TRADE
To locate your Harmonized System Tariff Number:
Census Bureau Foreign Trade Division
Importing into U.S. Customs Importers' Flash Facts
(202) 927-1692
Energy
Investment, Procurement Contracts
U.S. Dept. of Energy
(202) 586-6832; fax (202) 586-6148
Environment
General and the Border Environmental Cooperation
Commission
Environmental Protection Agency, NAFTA Task Force
(202) 260-6161; fax (202) 260-9459
Sanitary and Phytosanitary Measures under NAFTA:
EPA
(202) 260-2897; fax (202) 260-1847
Commercial Assistance on Environmental Issues: DOC
(202) 482-4152; fax (202) 482-5665

North American Development Bank: Dept. of Treasury
(202) 622-1850; fax (202) 622-0218
Government procurement
Canada
Office of Canada, DOC
(202) 482-3103; fax (202) 482-4729
Mexico
Office of Mexico DOC
(202) 482-0300; fax (202) 482-5865
NAFTA Government Procurement Provisions
Bureau of Economic and Business Affairs
Dept. of State
(202) 647-6683; fax (202) 647-6540
Investment
NAFTA Investment Provisions
Office of International Investment
Dept. of Treasury
(202) 622-1860; fax (202) 622-0391
Intellectual Property Rights
Intellectual Property Rights and NAFTA
Library of Congress
(202) 707-8350; fax (202) 707-6859
Patent and Trademark Office
(703) 305-9300; fax (703) 305-8885
Labor Issues
General NAFTA Issues
Dept. of Labor
(202) 501-6653; fax (202) 501-6615
Safeguards and Temporary Entry
Dept. of Labor
(202) 219-7597; fax (202) 219-5071
Marketing Information
NAFTA Facts
(202) 482-4464
New Exporter Information
NAFTA Facts
Canada—NAFTA FACTS
(202) 482-3101

Mexico—NAFTA FACTS
(202) 482-4464

Small Business Administration—International Trade
Programs
(202) 205-6720; fax (202) 208-7272

Trade Information Center
1-800-USA-TRADE
Services
Insurance in Mexico DOC
(202) 482-5261; fax (202) 482-4775

Other financial services
Dept. of Treasury
(202) 622-1986; fax (202) 622-1956

Other services
Office of Service Industries, DOC
(202) 482-5261; fax (202) 482-4775
Standards and Labelling
National Center for Standards and Certification Information
National Institute of Standards and Technology
(301) 975-4040; fax (301) 975-2128
Telecommunications
Offices of Telecommunications, DOC
(202) 482-4466; fax (202) 482-5834
Textiles and Apparel
Office of Textiles and Apparel, DOC
(202) 482-3400; fax (202) 482-2331

NAFTA FACTS
(202) 482-4464

U.S. Customs Flash Facts
(202) 927-1692
Transportation
Investment and Liberalization & U.S.-Mexico Cargo
Facilitation
Dept of Transportation
(202) 366-2892; fax (202) 366-7417

Land transportation
Office of Mexico, DOC

(202) 482-0300; fax (202) 482-5865
Rail transportation
Dept of Transportation
(202) 366-0354; fax (202) 366-7688
Safety standards
Dept. of Transportation
(202) 366-1790; fax (202) 366-7908
* State Agencies
Each State in the United States has an economic
development or commerce department that has information
on NAFTA.
* Private
Local Chambers of Commerce have information in varying
amounts
NAFTA Center, American Graduate School of
International Management, Glendale, Arizona
(602) 978-7194; fax: (602) 439-9622.
National Law Center for Inter-American Free Trade,
Tucson, Arizona
(602) 622-1200; fax: (602) 622-0957
World Trade Centers

Most of this information was obtained from the U.S. Department of Commerce publication, *The NAFTA Implementation Resource Guide,* February 18, 1994. Additional resources are listed in the guide.

So You're Working in Canada, the United States, and Mexico: Are You Prepared?

Several years ago, a group of recently returned expatriates who had lived two years or more abroad were asked this question, "What were some of the things you wished you had known when you were abroad that would have helped you work more effectively?"

One person said, "I wish I knew more about what the people are proud of, their writers and philosophers."

Another said, "I learned many of the basic courtesies too late."

This appendix information on Canada, the United States and Mexico is designed to fill this gap of knowledge and springboard the reader to further pursue the cultural aspects of each country.

Information on Canada

1. **There are many contemporary and historical people of whom a country is proud. Can you name one of each? Politician**

   Contemporary: Jean Chrétien (1934–). Prime Minister, Liberal Party.

   Historical: Lester Pearson (1897-1972). Prime Minister 1963-1968, Nobel Peace Prize, 1957.

Poet

Contemporary: Felix Leclerc (1914–). Accorded Member of Order of Canada and France's Chevalier of Légion of Honneur.

Historical: Stephen Leacock (1869–1944). Works include *Literary Lapses* (1920) and *Winnowwed Wisdom* (1926).

Philosopher

Contemporary: Pierre Berton (1920–). Perceptive historian and prolific writer. Most recent book is *The Arctic Grail* (1988).

Historical: Marshall McLuhan (1911–1981). Known for creating the aphorism "The medium is the message."

Musician

Contemporary: Joni Mitchell (1943–). Song writer and vocalist whose albums include *Mingus, Court and Spark,* and *Chalk Mark in a Rainstorm.*

Historical: Glenn Gould (1932–1982). Noted for his interpretations of Bach and the romantic composers.

Writer

Contemporary: Margaret Atwood (1939–). Novelist and poet. Her most current books include *Robber Bride* (1993), *Cat's Eye* (1988) and *The Handmaid's Tale* (1986).

Historical: Louis Hémon (1880–1913). French Canadian novelist journalist who wrote the classic *Maria Chapdelaine* (1911) translated by W.H. Blake.

Actor/Actress

Contemporary: John Candy (1951–1994). Winner of two Emmys. Comic actor whose films include *Uncle Buck,* and *Trains, Planes and Automobiles.*

Historical: Raymond Massey (1896–1983). Nominated for Academy Award for *Abe Lincoln in Illinois* and for his performance as Dr. Gillespie in the television series, *Dr. Kildare.*

Photographer

Contemporary:

Historical: Yousuf Karsh (1908–). Armenian immigrant. Noted portrait photographer of world leaders and celebrities.

Inventor

Contemporary: Chris Haney (1949?–). Along with John Haney and Scott Abbott created the board game Trivial Pursuit in 1979.

Historical: Dr. Frederick Banting (1891–1941). With John Macleod won the Nobel Prize in medicine (1921) and Charles Best for isolating the hormone insulin and advocating its use for diabetes.

Artist

Contemporary: David Milne (1882–1953). Painter, illustrator working in oils and watercolors. Works appeared in the Armory Show in New York, 1917.

Historical: Thomas Davies (late 1700s). Typographic artist whose art was reproduced in many early travel books.

Sports Figure

Contemporary: Elvis Stoiko (1974–). Silver medal for figure skating 1994 Winter Olympics, Lillehammer, Norway

Historical: Maurice "The Rocket" Richard (1921–) Montreal Canadian. Lifelong player who was the first to score 50 goals in a regular season. Career total 544 goals.

2. **Can you identify current political leaders and their titles?**
Prime Minister Jean Chrétien, Foreign Affairs Minister André Ouellet, Trade Minister Ray MacLaren, Industry Minister John Manley.

3. **Do you know the names of the political parties and their beliefs and functions?**
Progressive Conservative Party, Liberal Party, New Democratic Party founded 1961, Social Credit Party of Canada founded in 1930s, Independent.

4. **Is the payment of special fees (bribery) a part of the business system?**
No, special fees or bribes are not part of the Canadian business culture.

5. **Is the country divided into states, provinces, counties, or some other way? How many? Name them?**
Canada is a federation of ten provinces and two territories. The ten provinces are Quebec, Ontario, New Brunswick,

Manitoba, Nova Scotia, British Columbia, Saskatchewan, Prince Edward Island, Alberta, and Newfoundland. The two territories are Yukon Territory and the Northwest Territory.

6. **Are there any nonverbal behavior patterns you use that may be interpreted as "offensive?" (e.g., the A-OK gesture is obscene in Brazil).**
Nonverbal gestures that one would find offensive in the United States would most probably be found offensive in Canada.

7. **Can you anticipate some possible miscommunication problems?**
Those doing business with Canadians should be aware of the cultural groups, the English Canadians and French Canadians. The language and cultural complexity between these two groups does vary if one is uninformed of the differences.

8. **What are some routine courtesies one should observe?**
Canadians are more formal in their etiquette than Americans. A firm handshake and a sincere "hello" are appropriate greetings. Conversations are to the point, and farewells are short and friendly. Promptness is greatly appreciated. Men are expected to give up their seats on crowded buses to the elderly or women. When invited to one's home for dinner or when a gift is received, a letter of thanks is important.

9. **Is gift giving a custom? What kind of gift is appropriate for what particular occasion?**
On birthdays and Christmas, gifts are traditionally exchanged. When one is invited to the home of a Canadian, a bottle of wine, box of chocolates, or flowers are appropriate gifts for the host and/or hostess.

10. **How does religion influence the people?**
Most Canadians claim an affiliation with a particular religion, but active participation fluctuates. Fundamentalist are a small part of the religious makeup of Canada, and many Canadians are puzzled by the role of religion in U.S. politics. In Canada, it is legally acceptable to ask an individual his/her religious affiliation on a job application.

11. **What are the class divisions?**

    The upper class usually consists of those in leadership positions and with political power. The middle class is considered "classless" because the majority of the population fits into this category. Class divisions are also made by occupation. Physicians, lawyers, and corporate executives are in the upper class, while teachers, civil servants, clerks, and blue collar worker are considered middle class. Most of the upper and middle classes have a high standard of living, and there are very few desperately poor. There is upward mobility due to increased education, economic success, and specialized training.

12. **Is education free? Compulsory? How many years of attendance is required?**

    Education is a provincial responsibility. Attendance is required in the primary level from age 5–6 until ages 13–14. After primary, secondary education continues for three to five years. In some provinces, French-speaking students are entitled to instruction in French. Education is compulsory from ages 6 to 16. The federal government is responsible for education of the Indians and Eskimos.

13. **What are the most important elements of success? (e.g., salary, title, power)**

    When one wants to succeed one must have a good education, be trustworthy and ambitious, be able to motivate others, have perseverance, contacts and bilingual capability.

14. **What are some of the dominant business values? (e.g., competition)**

    Honesty, punctuality, courtesy, and formality head the list of dominant business values.

15. **Should you be "on time" or "late" for a business or social occasion?**

    It is important to be on time for business or social meetings.

16. **What kind of humor is understood and appreciated?**

    British humor, subtle and sarcastic, satire, and political jokes are enjoyed by most Canadians. Also, American humor characterized in American movies is appreciated.

Information on the United States

1. **There are many contemporary and historical people of whom a country is proud. Can you name one of each?**
Politician
Contemporary: Bill Clinton (1946–). President, Democratic party.
Historical: Abraham Lincoln (1809–1865). Sixteenth president of the United States during the Civil War.
Poet
Contemporary: Robert Frost (1874–1963). Pulitzer Prize in poetry 1924, 1931, 1937, and 1943. Poet Laureate during the Kennedy administration.
Historical: Walt Whitman (1819–1892). One of the greatest American poets. *Leaves of Grass* (1855) became one of the most influential volumes of poetry.
Philosopher
Contemporary: John Dewey (1859–1952). *Democracy and Education* influenced the structuring of free education for a democracy.
Historical: Thomas Paine (1737–1809). Wrote the pamphlet *Common Sense* during the American Revolution, plus 16 other pamphlets arguing for democratic institutions.
Musician
Contemporary: Billy Joel (1949–). Singer and song writer and entertainer. His albums include *Storm Front, Innocent Man, River of Dreams,* and *The Bridge.*
Historical: George Gershwin (1889–1937). Pulitzer Prize winner for *Of Thee I Sing,* (1931). Blended American traditional music with jazz and folk songs.
Writer
Contemporary: Toni Morrison (1931–). Pulitzer Prize winner for *Beloved* (1991). Her novels explore the black experience in a sparse and poetic style.
Historical: Mark Twain (1835–1910). *The Adventures of Tom Sawyer* and *Huckleberry Finn* are considered his masterpieces and reflect his boyhood on the Mississippi.

Actor/Actress

Contemporary: Clint Eastwood (1930–). Actor in American westerns and action movies. Also director and producer. Won an Academy Award for *The Unforgiven* (1993).

Historical: Helen Hayes (1910–1992). Referred to as the First Lady of the American Theater and starred in numerous movies.

Photographer

Contemporary: Ansel Adams (1902–1984). Photographed the American Southwest landscapes in sharp, superbly detailed black and white.

Historical: Dorthea Lange (1895–1965). Documentary photographs, most notably "Migrant Mother" (1936).

Inventor

Contemporary: Edwin H. Land (1909–1991). Invented the Polaroid camera and "instant" color photographs among others.

Historical: Thomas A. Edison (1847–1931). Prolific inventor, most notable for the incandescent lamp (1879).

Religious Leader

Contemporary: Billy Graham (1918–). Evangelical preacher who traveled internationally on evangelistic campaigns.

Historical: Mary Baker Eddy (1821–1910). Founder of the Christian Science movement. In 1908 she founded the *Christian Science Monitor,* a daily newspaper.

Artist

Contemporary: Georgia O'Keeffe (1887–1986). Her work is vibrant and abstract and represents motifs from the American Southwest.

Historical: Thomas Eakins (1844–1916). Considered the foremost American portraitist.

Sports Figure

Contemporary: Arnold Palmer (1929–). One of the most financially successful and victorious golfers in the history of golf.

Historical: Babe Ruth (1895–1948). The legend of the New York Yankees baseball team with his home run hits. He led the Yankees to seven pennants.

2. **Can you identify current political leaders and their titles?**
   President Bill Clinton, Vice President Al Gore, Secretary of State Warren Christopher, Speaker of the House Thomas Foley, Minority Leader in the Senate Robert Dole, Majority Leader in the Senate George Mitchell, Attorney General Janet Reno.

3. **Do you know the names of the political parties and their beliefs and functions?**
   The two major parties that have dominated United States politics since 1860 are the Republican and Democratic parties. The Democratic party traditionally represents the working class segment of American society. Being pro-labor it attempts to regulate policies at the federal level. The Republican party represents the business element and the enhancement of the business sector through little government involvement in business.

4. **Is the payment of special fees (bribery) a part of the business system?**
   The taking of bribes is illegal in the United States. Large corporations do employ lobbyists who work for favorable legislation in the Congress.

5. **Is the country divided into states, provinces, counties, or some other way? How many? Name them?**
   The United States is divided into 50 states and one district, the District of Columbia. There are approximately 3,044 counties.

6. **Are there any nonverbal behavior patterns you use that may be interpreted as "offensive?" (e.g., the A-OK gesture is obscene in Brazil).**
   American non-verbal communication is fairly straightforward.

7. **Can you anticipate some possible miscommunication problems?**
   American discussions are generally frank and open. Americans are comfortable with a speaking distance that

is approximately 32 inches. In more formal situations, one might increase the distance. Americans do not like to be touched when in conversation. They do make direct eye contact and find it disconcerting when the person they are talking with does not.

8. **What are some routine courtesies one should observe?**
Americans are informal in their greetings. They generally greet each other with a firm handshake and "hello." They may call a person by his or her first name after one meeting. Farewells are short and may end with "Take care," "See you," "Take it easy," or "Good-bye" and a friendly handshake. When dining, one does not talk with food in the mouth or place elbows on the table.

9. **Is gift giving a custom? What kind of gift is appropriate for what particular occasion?**
Gift giving is customary on birthdays and Christmas and family occasions (anniversaries, etc.). When one is invited for dinner a bottle of wine, flowers, or candy are acceptable gifts. Generally, today strong alcoholic beverages are avoided because many Americans are health conscious. Greeting cards are sometimes given when one does not know the other person too well but wants to acknowledge a special day or holiday.

10. **How does religion influence the people?**
A majority of religions in the United States are based on Judeo-Christian teachings. These religions determine moral guidelines that oftentimes carry over into politics. The abortion issue is the most widely publicized example of this. Church attendance in the United States is very common.

11. **What are the class divisions?**
There is an upper, middle, and lower class and these divisions are most commonly made by financial criteria. Education is viewed as a possible way to become upwardly mobile and to increase one's position in society. The upper class is generally composed of professional people or those who have inherited great wealth. The middle class is a strong and resilient element of American society. The lower class is composed of a large number of minorities.

12. **Is education free? Compulsory? How many years of attendance is required?**
American education is a free and public institution. Attendance is compulsory from ages 7 to 16. The education system is administered by the local and state governments, with some funds provided by the federal government.

13. **What are the most important elements of success? (e.g., salary, title, power)**
The most important elements are ambition and ability. If one possesses these, then generally the salary, power, and title follow.

14. **What are some of the dominant business values? (e.g., competition, etc.)**
Generally, Americans value competitiveness and are often motivated by it. Along this line, Americans can be assertive and dedicated. Most believe in hard work and fair play.

15. **Should you be "on time" or "late" for a business or social occasion?**
For a business appointment, one should be on time. You may have to wait briefly for your contact person, but schedules and appointments are adhered to. For social occasions, one may be 15 minutes late and still be considered on time. If one is going to be later than that, a telephone call to alert the host/hostess is appreciated.

16. **What kind of humor is understood and appreciated?**
Americans enjoy their comic strips in the daily newspapers as well as political cartoons and jokes. Americans find amusing events in their everyday lives that one is able to twist into a humorous antidote or sarcasm. The ability to laugh at oneself and not take yourself too seriously is important. Some Americans enjoy harmful practical jokes.

Information on Mexico

1. **There are many contemporary and historical people of whom a country is proud, Can you name one of each? Politician:**
Contemporary: President Carlos Salinas de Gortari (1945–).

Historical: Benito Juarez (1806–1872). One of the greatest Mexican leaders responsible for leading his country in the war for independence.

Poet

Contemporary: Armado Nervo (1879–1919). Prolific writer of poetry and fiction analyzing the psychological and philosophical nature of a personal dilemma.

Historical: Sor Juana Inés de la Cruz (1648–1695). Mexico's first woman writer/poet. A nun who wrote the well-known philosophical poem entitled "First Dream," *Primer Sueño.*

Philosopher

Contemporary: Octavio Paz (1914–). Nobel Prize (1990). First Mexican to receive the award. Considered one of the great intellects of postwar Mexico.

Historical: Alfonso Reyes (1889–). Charter member of Ateneo de la Juventud, who wrote and campaigned for educational and ideological reform during 1910–1920.

Musician

Contemporary: Carlos Chavez (1899–1978). He organized the first permanent symphony in Mexico and is considered one of the most illustrious persons in 20th-century Mexican music.

Historical: Manuel Ponce (1882–1948). Pianist and composer. His music reflects his interest in Mexican native folk music. He was the teacher of Carlos Chavez.

Writer

Contemporary: Carlos Fuentes (1928–). One of Mexico's best known writer's of fiction. Ambassador to France 1975–1977.

Historical: Mariano Azuela (1873–1952). Physician for Pancho Villa's army. Wrote one of the first books about the Revolution (1910–1917) entitled *Los de abajo (The Underdogs).*

Actor/Actress

Contemporary: Silvia Pinal (1938–). Well known stage and screen actress and producer of musical comedies.

Historical: Maria Felix (1914–) "La Dona." One of the true legends created by the Mexican cinema.

Inventor

Contemporary: Luis Enrique Erro (1897–1955). Scientist and founder of the National Astrophysics Observatory in 1941.

Religious Leader

Historical: Father Miguel Hidalgo (1753–1811). Mexican priest who is called "The Father of the Mexican Revolution."

Artist

Contemporary: David Alfaro Siqueiros (1886–1959). Muralist, painter, and graphic artist. His career was divided between painting and his revolutionary activities. *Historical:* Diego Rivera (1886–1957). Famous Mexican muralist whose murals dealt symbolically with Mexican social issues.

Sports Figure

Contemporary: Fernando Valenzuela (1960–). Pitcher for the Los Angeles Dodgers. *Historical:* Carlos Alberto Torres.

2. **Can you identify current political leaders and their titles?**

President Carlos Salinas de Gortari, Minister of Foreign Relations Fernando Solana Morales, Minister of Finance and Public Credit Dr. Pedro Aspe Armella, Minister of the Interior, Jose Gonzalez Garrida.

3. **Do you know the names of the political parties and their beliefs and functions?**

The PRI (Partido Revolucionario Institucional), the Institutional Revolutionary Party, was founded in 1929. It draws its support from workers and peasants being broadly based and moderately left.

The PAN (Partido de Accion Nacional), The National Action Party, was founded in 1939 and developed its conservative reaction to PRI's anti-clerical, anti-business policies.

4. **Is the payment of special fees (bribery) a part of the business system?**

Bribery (*mordida,* "the bite") is very common in Mexico. The old traditions of favor and patronage begun by influential Mexican families has extended to business and politics, and many bureaucracies are involved in the payments of "special fees."

5. **Is the country divided into states, provinces, counties, or some other way? How many? Name them?**
Mexico is divided into 32 states and one federal district.

6. **Are there any nonverbal behavior patterns you use that may be interpreted as "offensive?" (e.g., the A-OK gesture is obscene in Brazil).**
The same offensive nonverbal gestures that apply in the United States apply in Mexico.

7. **Can you anticipate some possible miscommunication problems?**
Miscommunication may occur regarding the different perceptions of time, physical contact, and physical space between speakers.

8. **What are some routine courtesies one should observe?**
Etiquette is more formal in Mexico than in the U.S. Men open doors and pull out chairs for women. Superiors are addressed by the formal form of you (*usted*). Men greet each other with a handshake in the business situation. If one is friends with a Mexican, an embrace or kiss on the cheek is appropriate.

9. **Is gift giving a custom? What kind of gift is appropriate for what particular occasion?**
When one is invited for dinner, one can appropriately bring flowers, wine, or candy, although Mexican folklore has it that yellow flowers signify death. Giving a gift in a business context is not required but if one does choose to do so, a small gift with your company logo is a good choice. Gifts are generally opened in the presence of the giver. Gifts of silver are not considered appropriate for Mexicans.

10. **How does religion influence the people?**
The Roman Catholic Church traditionally has played a great role in the formation of Mexican culture and continues to influence the Mexican daily life today.

11. What are the class divisions?

The class divisions in Mexico are polarized and great disparities exist between the upper class and lower class. Approximately 40 percent of the nation's income goes to the richest 10 percent of the population, while the lowest 10 percent live in absolute poverty. Social rank is determined by birth, and it is very difficult to move upward socially.

12. Is education free? Compulsory? How many years of attendance is required?

Education in Mexico is both free and compulsory from ages 6 through 15.

13. What are the most important elements of success? (e.g., salary, title, power)

Success in Mexico is measured first by one's title, then power, and then by financial situation. Education and obtaining a title is important to the middle class, while land ownership is significant to the lower class.

14. What are some of the dominant business values? (e.g., competition, etc.)

As Mexico becomes more industrialized, competition has gained greater importance. Also of importance, is the understanding of hierarchial power structures, personal contacts, and a conciliatory relationship with the government. Business people are expected to be trustworthy and hard working.

15. Should you be "on time" or "late" for a business or social occasion?

Generally, one should strive to be on time, although invitations might specify a particular date but are sometimes vague about the specific time. One should not necessarily expect one's Mexican counterpart to be on time or expect an apology if he/she is late. When invited to a Mexican home, it is expected that guests will be at least an hour late.

16. What kind of humor is understood and appreciated?

Puns on words, jokes about the government, as well as other kinds of humor are appreciated.

Bibliography

"Across the Boarder," *Utne Reader*, January/February 1993.

Adler, Nancy J., *International Dimensions of Organizational Behavior*, Boston: PWS-Kent Publishing Company, 1991.

American Chamber of Commerce of Mexico, *Guide to Mexico for Business*, Mexico City, Mexico, 1992.

Baker, George, "Secrets for Being a Real Person in Spanish," *Business Mexico*, October 1992.

Bamrud, Joachim, "North America, Inc.," *U.S./Latin Trade*, January 1994.

Barnhart, Katherine, "A Canadian Thumbs Up for the NAFTA?" *Business Mexico*, October 1992.

Barrett, John K., *American Competitiveness in Mexico Under the North American Free Trade Agreement*, Harvard University, June 1993.

Bayne, Clive Alexander, "Strategies for Developing Business English Writing Skills," *Business Mexico*, September 1988.

Borrego, Rene, "Signposts for Regional Investment," *Business Mexico*, March 1992.

Bubrick, George J., "Results-Based Management: A Success Formula for the 90s," *Business Mexico*, March 1992.

Cambio 16 America, No. 1.141, October 4, 1993.

"Canada—An Investment Perspective," *Investment Canada*, 1990.

Cancelada, Gregory D., "Southern Strategy: Mexico Pushes Free Trade South," *Business Mexico*, March 1991.

Carlsen, Laura, "Modernization and Maturity," *Business Mexico*, September 1991.

Carlsen, Laura, "NAFTA: A Change for the Better?" *Business Mexico*, March 1992.

Carlsen, Laura, "Participating in Productivity," *Business Mexico*, September 1991.

Carlsen, Laura, "Making Changes . . . ," *Business Mexico*, September 1991.

Carlsen Laura., "Mexican labor in the 90's," *Business Mexico*, November 1991.

Carlsen, Laura, "A Common Goal," *Business Mexico*, September 1991.

Castaned, Jorge G., "The Fury Finds an Outlet," *Newsweek*, January 17, 1994.

Castonguay, Gilles, "Testing the Waters: Canadian Investors Look (Tentatively) at Mexico," *Business Mexico*, Special Edition 1992.

Centeno, Miguel Angel and Maxfield, Sylvia, "The Marriage of Finance and order: Changes in the Mexican Political Elite," *J. Lat. Am. Stud.*

Cesar, Jose Joaquin; Guaida, Luis Manuel; Lara, Fernando; De Regil, Jorge, "Keep It a Secret But . . . The Reduced Work Shift Could Be a Contributing Factor in the Solution of the Economic Crisis," *Business Mexico*, March 1988.

Competing in the Workplace," *Business Mexico*, September 1991.

Current, Williams, Freidel, *American History, A Survey*, New York, Alfred A. Knopf, Inc., 1979.

deForest, Mariah, "Quality Has to Be Learned," *Business Mexico*, March 1988.

"Demographics of North America," *The Conference Board*, 1986.

Dudley, James W., *1992: Strategies for the Single Market*, London, Kogan Page, 1990.

Elashmawi, Farid & Harris, Philip R., *Multicultural Management, New Skills for Global Success*, Houston: Gulf Publishing Co., 1993.

"El Poder Femenino: el poder del trabajo," *Medico Moderno*, November 1993.

Emerson, Ralph Waldo, *Emerson, Essays: First and Second Series*, U.S.A., Vintage Books, 1990.

Export U.S.A., *Export Programs and Services,* U.S. Department of Commerce, January 1992.

Farquharson, Mary, "Solidarity Salinas-Style," *Business Mexico,* October 1991.

Farquharson, Mary, "Maquila Conundrum," *Business Mexico,* September 1991.

Farver, Deena, "Benchmarking, the Lesson: Learn From the Leaders," *Business Mexico,* November 1992.

Fenley, Lindajoy, "NAFTA Talks Advance in Mexico," *Business Mexico,* December 1991.

"Foreign Investment in NAFTA: A U.S. Perspective," *Business Mexico,* Special Edition 1992.

Foster, Lynn V. and Foster Lawrence, *1991 Mexico, U.S.A.,* Fielding Travel Books, 1991.

Fraser, Dave, "Canada's Negotiable Hot Spots," *Business Mexico,* March 1992.

Fraser, Dave, "The Benefits of Trilateral Free Trade," *Business Mexico,* March 1992.

Fromson, Derek, "When is a Rose Not a Rose?" *Business Mexico,* October 1992.

Garcia, Robert Newell, "Two Things to Cheer About," *Business Mexico,* March 1987.

Garza, Hernando, "Siguen vivos los 'guercos' y las 'sias'," *El Norte,* Section D, September 20, 1993.

Geyer, Anne, "Industry Goes to School," *Business Mexico,* April 1992.

Gilbreath, Kent, "A Businessman's Guide to the Mexican Economy," *Columbia Journal of World Business,* vol XXI, number 2.

Gramma, "The Biggest Robbery of the 19th Century: Bast YA," *Informational News Forum for the Liberation of La Roza,* April 1972.

Grayson, George W., "A Love—Hate Relationship with North America," *National Negotiating Styles,* Foreign Service Institute, U.S. Department of State, April 1987.

Greider, William, "National Affairs, Congress: Kill NAFTA," *Rolling Stone,* October 28, 1993.

Hall, Russ, "Profile of an Investor," *Business Mexico,* Special Edition 1992.

Harris, P.R. and Moran, R.T., *Managing Cultural Differences,* Houston: Gulf Publishing Company, 1991.

Hernandez, Maria Eugenia, "Financing Franchises," *Business Mexico,* December 1991.

Hevrdejs, Judy, "Storming The Windy City," *Business Mexico,* May 1991.

Hudson, Brendan, "NAFTA Update," *Business Mexico,* October 1991.

Hudson, Brendan, "Business and the Law, The Background for NAFTA Dispute Resolution," *Business Mexico,* November 1991.

"If the US-Mexican Talks Are Going So Well, Why So Much Anxiety?" *Latin American Weekly Report,* February 6, 1992.

I.T.E.S.M. and Bancomext, *Diplomado en Exportacion,* 1993.

ILT Mexico, "Mexico," *Business International Corp,* August 1989.

Informe Anual al Personal 1993, Vitro, 1994.

"Intrafirm Trade and the New North American Business Dynamic," *The Conference Board of Canada,* Report 88-92, 1992.

"Investment in Economic Development, 1980–1989," *Atlas Nacional de Mexico,* UNAM, 1991.

Jauregui, Miguel, "Free Trade Agreement: The Mexican legislative Process," *Business Mexico,* July 1991.

Jaynes, Gerald David & Williams Jr., Robin M., *A Common Destiny, Blacks and American Society,* Washington, D.C., National Academy Press, 1989.

Kelso, Laura, "Free Trade Unveiled," *Business Mexico,* December 1992.

Kennedy, Paul, *Preparing for the Twenty-First Century,* New York, Random House, 1993.

"Keeping an Eye on the NAFTA Line," *U.S. News & World Report,* November 8, 1993.

Kleiner, Pangola, "Hay espacio en el para los negros?" *Medico Moderno,* November 1993.

Knight, Alan, "The Peculiarities of Mexican History: Mexico Compared to Latin America, 1821–1992," *J. Lat. Amer. Stud. Supplement.*

Kootnikoff, Lawrence, "The Vision of Carlos Salinas de Gortari," *U.S./Latin Trade,* January 1994.

Krugman, Paul R., "NAFTA: An Empty Victory?" *U.S. News & World Report,* November 29, 1993.

Kurtzman, Joel, *The Decline and Crash of the American Economy,* New York: W.W. Norton & Company, 1988.

Lamont, Robert, "Eleven Tips for Selling Letters," *Business Mexico,* June 1988.

Lande, Stephen, "From Protection to Free Trade," *Business Mexico,* July 1991.

"Las 500 Empresas mas Importantes de Mexico," *Expansion,* August 18,1993.

Leon, Roberto Salinas, "Talk with a Free-Trader," *Business Mexico,* August 1992.

Lewicki, Roy J. & Litterer, Joseph A., *Negotiation,* Homewood, Illinois Irwin, 1985.

Lipset, Martin, "Culture and Economic Behavior: A Commentary," *Journal of Labor Economics,* 1993, vol. 11, no. 1.

Loeb, Marshall & Kirkland, Richard, "Clinton Speaks on the Economy," *Fortune,* August 23, 1993.

Lopez, Laura, "The Angry Youths Behind the Masks," *Time,* February 7, 1994.

Luxner, Larry, "Mexico Reaches for New Telecom Heights," *Telephony,* February 3, 1992.

MacDonald, Christine, "Silicon Valley South, Guadalajara Braces for the Future," *Business Mexico,* July 1992.

MacDonald, Christine, "Monterrey: Free Trade Without a Treaty," *Business Mexico,* June 1992.

MacDonald, Christine, "Gamesa Heat," *Business Mexico,* March 1991.

Malnight, Thomas W., "Sabritas 1991," *Harvard Business School,* October 25, 1991.

"Major Highways, Vegetation, Ecological Regions," *Atlas Nacional de Mexico,* UNAM, 1991.

Mansell, Alice Jean, "Books," *Business Mexico,* July 1991, p. 49.

McCarthy, Donald, "Antidote to Optimism," *Business Mexico,* April 1992.

Margain-Santos-Gonzalez-Vargas, S.C., *Main Legal Aspects of Doing Business in Mexico,* Monterrey, Mexico.

Margain-Santos-Rojas-Gonzalez-Vargas, *Aspects of Doing Business in Mexico,* Monterrey, Mexico.

Martinez, Fernando Fernandez, *Curriculum Vitae,* November 1993.

EuroNotas, July 1993.

McCarthy, Donald, "Do the Right Thing, Business Mexico Review," *Business Mexico,* March 1992.

McCarthy Donald, "An Ariadne for NAFTA Observers," *Business Mexico,* July 1992.

McCarthy, Donald, "Ford Accelerates in Mexico," *Business Mexico,* September 1991.

McDonald, Marci, "Portrait of Two Nations," *McLean's,* June 25, 1990.

Malcolm, A.H., *The Canadians,* New York: Books/Random House, 1985.

"Mexico Integration, Nafta Could Be Ready in Weeks," *Latin American Weekly Report,* February 20, 1992.

"Mexico, Economy, Beyond the Jitters at US Court Ruling," *Latin American Weekly Report,* October 14, 1993.

"Mexico, Politics, Reform Mark II Is Now in Place," *Latin American Weekly Report,* September 30, 1993.

"Mexico, Trade, Already No. 2 Market for US," *Latin American Weekly Report,* June 3, 1993.

"Mexico, Trade, Talks with US and Canada Heat Up," *Latin American Weekly Report,* January 23, 1992.

"Mexico, Trade and Diplomacy, The Details of the Parallel Agreements," *Latin American Weekly Report,* September 2, 1993.

Morales, Jose S. Mendez, *Problemas Economicos de Mexico,* Mexico, McGraw Hill, 1991.

Moran, Robert T., Harris, Philip R., Stripp, William G., *Developing the Global Organization,* Houston: Gulf Publishing, 1993.

Morris, Charles R., *The Coming Global Boom,* U.S.A.: Bantam Books, 1990.

Mundo Maya, Vol.2 No.1, Summer–Fall 1993.

"NAFTA: Texas Builds Its Future," The Dallas Morning News, December 26, 1993, Section P.

"NAFTA, Who's Next?" *U.S./Latin Trade,* January 1994.

Observador internacional, Year 1, No. 9, August 23, 1993.

Official Canadian NAFTA Brochure, 1993

Orme, William A Jr., *Continental Shift: Free Trade and the New North America,* Washington, D.C., The Washington Post Company, 1993.

Padgett, Tim, "Rage of the Zapatistas," *Newsweek,* January 17, 1994.

Padgett, Tim, "The Pervasive Craft of Graft?" *Newsweek,* May 17, 1993.

Paz, Octavio, *El Laberinto de la Soledad, Pastdata, Vuelta a El Laberinto de la Soledad,* Mexico D.F., Fondo de Cultura Economica, 1993.

Pazos, Luis, *Free Trade: Mexico-U.S.A. Myths and Facts,* Mexico, Diana, 1991.

Pocket Facts: Canada—Economic Indicators, Source: Statistics Canada, Number 20, May 15, 1992.

Pocket Facts: Canada—Economic Indicators, Source: Statistics Canada, Number 25, July 15, 1993.

"Politics and Media, Scandal over Radio Censorship," *Latin American Weekly Report,* October 14, 1993.

"Population and Area, By State," *Censo General de Poblacion y Vivienda,* 1990.

Porche, Mike, "Companies and Universities—Joint Venture Partners in Learning," *Business Mexico,* June 1987.

Quezada, Sergio Aguayo, "TLC: el mito y la esperanza," *el Norte,* November 6, 1993.

Ramos, Jorge, "Espanglish...? o que es esto que hablamos?" *El Norte,* Section D, page 6, November 3, 1993.

Ramsamooj, Derek, "Japan in Mexico: Taking the Long View," *Business Mexico,* May 1991.

Ramsamooj, Derek, "Japan in Mexico: Foreign Investment," *Business Mexico,* June 1991.

Reich, Robert B., *The Work of Nations,* New York: Vintage Books, 1992.

Riding, Alan, *Distant Neighbors, A Portrait of the Mexicans,* U.S.A.: Vintage Books, 1989.

Roberts, Steven B., "Forward Ho, After NAFTA," *U.S. News & World Report,* November 29, 1993.

Russell, Joel, "Fleshing Out a Skeleton Treaty," *Business Mexico,* July 1992.

Russell, Joel, "Hemispheric Vision: David Rockefeller Shares His Dream of Free Trade in the Americas," *Business Mexico,* August 1992.

Ryan, Jodi, "Striving for the Best," *Business Mexico,* May 1992.

Ryan, Jodi, "A New Era in the North American Relationship," *Business Mexico,* April 1992.

Salinas, Roberto, "Privatizacion en Mexico: Buena, pero Insuficiente," *Backgrounder,* Washington D.C., The Heritage Foundation, No. 41, June 28, 1991.

Salinas, Roberto, "Privatization in Mexico: Much Better, but Still Not Enough," *Backgrounder,* Washington, D.C., The Heritage Foundation, No. 172, January 20, 1992.

Scott, Robert E., *Mexican Government in Transition,* Chicago, University of Illinios Press, 1971.

Secretaria de Fomento Industrial y Comercial, *Nuevo Leon, Mexico: Land of Investment Opportunity.*

Silverstein, Jeff, "Some Mexican Firms Can't Wait for Free Trade Pact," *San Francisco Chronicle,* February 17, 1992, Section B.

Silverstein, Jeff, "Monterrey Industrialists Prepare to Enter U.S. Market," *Business Mexico,* March 1992.

Silverstein, Jeff, "Passing the NAFTA, Scenarios for U.S. Legislative Action," *Business Mexico,* May 1992.

Silverstein, Jeff, "Monterrey Cleans Up, Corporations Take the Lead," *Business Mexico,* May 1992.

Sinclair, Robert, *Industrial Competitiveness and Culture in Monterrey,* ITESM Centro de Sistemas de Manufactura, June 1993.

Smith, T. Bradbrooke, "The Canadian Treaty Making and Implementation Process," *Business Mexico,* November 1991.

Smith, Wesley R., "Protecting the Environment in North America with Free Trade," *Backgrounder,* The Heritage Foundation, Washington D.C., No.889, April 2, 1992.

Smith, Wesley R., "Salinas Prepara la Agricultura Mexicana para el Comercio Libre," *Backgrounder,* The Heritage Foundation, Washington D.C., No. 46, October 30, 1992.

Smith, Wesley R., "U.S. Needs 'NAFTA Czar' to Promote Free Trade in the Americas," *The Heritage Foundation,* Executive Memorandum #323, Washington D.C., February 13, 1992.

Smith, Wesley, "Guidelines for U.S. Negotiators at the Trade Talks with Mexico," *Backgrounder,* The Heritage Foundation, Washington D.C., No. 861, October 18, 1991.

Stoddard, Ellwyn R., *Maquila, Assembly Plants in Northern Mexico,* El Paso, Texas Western Press, 1988.

"Stretching Tenors," *Latin Finance,* No.51, November 1993.

The Berkeley Guides, *On the Loose in Mexico,* U.S.A., Fodor's Travel Publications, 1993.

"The New Face of America," *Time: Special Issue,* Fall 1993.

Thurow, Lester, *Head to Head,* New York: Warner Books, 1993.

"Top Industries by Employment," INEGI 1989.

Tromben, Carlos, "Los que abren las puertas," *AmericaEconomia,* April 1993.

"Trade and Diplomacy, For Salinas, Nafta Is Top Priority," *Latin American Weekly Report,* March 4, 1993.

Tully, Shawn, "The Real key to Creating Wealth," *Fortune,* September 20, 1993.

U.S. Embassy, *Servicios que Proporciona el Servicio de Comercio Exterior de los E.E.U.U. a los Empresarios Mexicanos,* September 9, 1992.

U.S./Latin Trade, January 1994.

U.S. Foreign Commercial Service, *Servicios que proporciona a la Comunidad de negocios mexicana el Servicio Exterior del Departamento de Comercio de los E.E.U.U.,* February 1988.

U.S.A., *List of Services and Fees U.S. & Foreign Commercial Service Mexico,* 1992.

Watling, John, "Improving Productivity," *Business Mexico,* August 1992.

West, Cornel, *Race Matters,* Boston: Beacon Press, 1993.

White House, "NAFTA: The Beginning of a New Era," *Business America,* August 24, 1992.

Wientraub, Sidney, "Jobs on the Line," *Business Mexico,* March 1991.

Wilson, Michael G. and Smith, Wesley R., "The North American Free Trade Agreement: Spurring Prosperity and Stability in the

Americas," *The Heritage Lectures,* Washington D.C.: Heritage
Foundation Conference, 1992.

Witoshynsky, Mary, "Total Quality: A Strategy for Success,"
Business Mexico, October 1991.

Zuckerman, Mortimer B., "It's the Global Economy, Stupid," *U.S.
News & World Report,* August, 9, 1993.

Index